*I am a product of opportunity meeting preparation and countless people believing and investing in me. I am eternally thankful for my family and friends who have stood with me and championed me over the years.*

*This book is for people who I may never meet face to face. I hope what you glean from its contents helps you to go further than I ever could. In the words of C. S. Lewis...*

*"Go further up, and further in."*

# KELLY CLARK

# INSPIRED

## PURSUIT OF PROGRESS

SPARROW PUBLISHING

# CONTENTS

# ENDORSEMENTS

Kelly's record-breaking snowboarding wins have inspired us all. Now she inspires us in a whole new way with her first book about why winning isn't everything. Focusing on what you can give instead of what you can get is a valuable lesson we can all learn from Kelly's story.

Jake Burton
*Founder of Burton Snowboards*

I've known Kelly since she was a teenager, and I've had a front-row seat to many of the triumphs and challenges she so candidly describes in *Inspired*. It is rare for an athlete to reach the pinnacle of achievement in their teens; and rarer still for them to make it through the resulting chaos and disillusionment with any real sense of self. Kelly did both. Through honest reflection and unwavering conviction, Kelly refused to define herself by her competitive results, and through her search for what is real, managed to find the true beauty in snowboarding, life, and most importantly, herself. Ironically, over the course of this amazing journey, she just so happened to become one of the winningest athletes in all of sport! This book should be required reading for all young athletes, not to help them achieve success, but rather so they can better understand what it really is.

Peter Carlisle
*Managing Director of Olympics & Action Sports, Octagon*

Words of wisdom from an elite athlete, *Inspired* offers the reader tools to unlock the motivation and mindsets that reside within. Goal-oriented and determined, Kelly is not only the most winning competitor in the history of snowboarding; she is also driven to be consistent in all areas of life. Kelly shares insight and thoughtful questions into how we may all benefit from showing up consistently in our lives, even when we may not feel like it.

Susie Floros
*Editor in Chief,* Snowboard *Magazine, former Burton Women's Team Manager*

The hallmark of Kelly Clark's remarkable snowboarding career is not that she has won more contests than any other athlete—it is that she has done so while remaining authentic, committed and true to her core belief that anything is possible. Along her journey, Clark figured out her "why," her motivation to consistently push beyond previous limits. By sharing her stories, earned over two decades of professional snowboarding, she hopes to inspire the next generation of doers to discover their "why" and continue shifting the limits of possibility.

Alyssa Roenigk
*ESPN Senior Writer, Author of* The Tao of Travis Pastrana

I recognize Kelly as a mighty one. It is not about what she has done on the snowboard. It is about how she lives her life. I admire Kelly for her grit, her mindset and her work ethic. There is no luck in what she has achieved in her life. What I love most about Kelly is her huge heart. She lives beyond herself. She lives with purpose and light. She believes in kindness and in helping people. She believes she can make a difference. And belief is everything. I am grateful to be a part of her journey.

Torah Bright
*Olympic Gold and Silver Medalist*

There's a secret that snowboarding really parallels life and success. As the founder of STOKED, a national youth mentoring program that uses sports like snowboarding to teach leadership and success skills to youth, this book really resonates with me and the work I've done over 12 years with adults and youth. This isn't your typical success and motivation book. This is a personal account of the ups and downs of one of the most successful athletes of our generation. I appreciate the honesty, vulnerability, and insight Kelly shares. Kelly writes about how leading with your "why" can help you create a long career, how actually letting go of expectation can lead to extraordinary results, and how to embrace the process of the journey you're on. Kelly illustrates the power of preparation and being internally motivated to accomplish your biggest goals. *Inspired* isn't about inspiration; it's a roadmap to living the life you want. This powerful book empowers, motivates, and propels you to prepare for the important "30 seconds" of your life, whether it is being an olympic athlete, starting a business, or changing the world.

Steve Larosiliere
*Founder & President STOKED*

I have known Kelly since she was 15 and have watched her go from a talented young snowboarder to Olympic champion. *Inspired* is a detailed outline on how to find daily fulfillment in reaching for the loftiest goals. Kelly's commitment to enjoying the process and constantly redefining success is what has kept her at the top of the sport for nearly two decades. I would say this book is a must-read for any serious athlete.

Rick Bower
*Head Halfpipe Coach U.S. Snowboard Team*

Kelly and I grew up in snowboarding together as one another's closest friends and also one another's biggest competitors—a rare feat indeed! Of course I'm proud of Kelly for all she's achieved in snowboarding and for now completing another dream in the completion of this book. And I'm even prouder of the human being she has become through this process. We're lucky that she's chosen to share her gems with us.

Gretchen Bleiler
*Olympic & X Games Medalist*

I've known a few people who I can say are consistent champions on and off the stage. Kelly Clark is one of these rare individuals. I met her over a decade ago and have lived impressed by her ever since. There are a series of lessons and challenges that are the secret driving this woman to be who she is to so many. I highly recommend that you read *Inspired* with the expectation that you will learn to live a truly championship life.

Danny Silk
*President, Loving on Purpose*


I can think of no one better than Kelly Clark to write a book on what success is really about and what motivates us. For someone who has dominated her profession for years and yet struggled with the definition of success, she is in a unique position to share the lessons she's learned in her own life. Kelly challenges us like only she can, with profound authenticity, to look again at what is motivating us and where we find success. *Inspired* will take you on a journey to re-examine the beliefs you hold that are hindering you while showing you the path to a fulfillment that goes beyond what you do and into who you are.

Banning Liebscher
*Jesus Culture Founder and Pastor*
*Author of* Rooted: The Hidden Places Where God Develops You


When I was first given *Inspired*, I read it ravenously and finished it in 36 hours. This book not only put into words many of my own thoughts and experiences as a professional athlete, but also incited me to see my profession with new eyes of vision and purpose. Anyone striving for new levels of excellence in their sphere of influence will find here a wealth of wisdom and inspiration.

Sara Hall
*Professional Marathoner and Co-Founder of The Hall Steps Foundation*

Kelly Clark has chosen a path few choose to take. From a young age, she has excelled both as an athlete and as a human being. I believe every person should read *Inspired* and find in its pages keys and insights to save years of frustration and heartache. Kelly has cracked the code of thriving and living in a world based on performance and expectations. Whether pursuing purpose in life or striving for significance, let this book permeate the way you think and view every situation. You will begin to find meaning in the mundane and get a new perspective to see trials and obstacles as opportunities for growth. No matter what, you will be changed.

Eric Johnson
*Author & Speaker*


This is not a normal book because Kelly Clark is not a normal woman. I remember visiting her with friends to watch her second Olympic qualifier tournament, and to watch Kelly is to watch a phenomenon. Behind the scenes though, Kelly is just as striking and her solid life perspective is so contagious; this book is not only going to do what its title says for you, but it needed to be written by someone like Kelly who shares from her unique life perspective. Hearing from someone who has had the success she has in her career and studying her process is invaluable, and as you read it you won't see any distance between yourself and Kelly. She takes huge subjects of performance, the struggle of success, fear, transition, and breaks them down through her own vulnerable stories and perspective so that you aren't just on her journey with her, but you feel like she is on your journey with you! Read this book and let the process of a world champion become your own!

Shawn Bolz
*Author of* Translating God, God Secrets, Growing Up with God
*TV Personality and Minister*
*www.bolzministries.com*

Kelly's commitment to set goals, pursue personal growth, and steward her calling for the benefit of others is a map from which every one of us will benefit. Every person who has a dream should read this book to find true inspiration from someone who has lived a life of purpose.

Gabe Lyons
*Author and President of Qs*

Kelly Clark is a world-class athlete who has pushed past her fears to embrace her divine destiny. Her book *Inspired* will challenge you to live fully actualized and completely alive. Kelly's book reads like an action movie in which her own life stories test the boundaries of the human spirit. As you venture deep into *Inspired* you will find yourself tempted to stand up on your chair and start cheering. It's just that good! If you are bored with life or overcome with complacency and you need something to jolt you into a new reality, this book is for you! Kelly will jump-start your future and launch you into your divine purpose. I highly recommend this book.

Kris Vallotton
*Leader, Bethel Church, Redding, CA*
*Co-Founder of Bethel School of Supernatural Ministry*
*Author of twelve books, including* The Supernatural Ways of Royalty, Heavy Rain and Destined to Win

I know very few people who work just as hard on reaching their external goals as they do their internal goals. I have always admired Kelly's determination and humility. Kelly's book *Inspired* will challenge and encourage the reader to not just go after the dreams in their heart, but to build a life that leaves a legacy even greater than their accomplishments! If you want to cultivate something that will last, this book is for you!

Kim Walker Smith
*Singer, Songwriter, Jesus Culture*

Kelly is one of the most mentally tough individuals I know. Her athletic career alone is enough to inspire. This book not only sheds light on her success but also on the process she has taken to maintain and pursue such a high level of excellence on and off of snow. Her simplistic approach to complex circumstances will inspire and provide you with the tools to change your own lens and live on purpose.

Dr. Lauren Loberg
*Sport Psychology Consultant*

# ACKNOWLEDGMENTS

I reference it many times in the book, but I would like to first and foremost thank my parents, Terry and Cathy Clark, for believing in me and being living examples of what is possible through hard work. Without the foundation you gave me growing up, this book would not have anything to stand on—neither would I.

I am not sure I would have survived, much less written a book, if it were not for my friends and family who took care of me post-hip surgery. A special thanks to my brother, Tim, AKA "Mr. Mom," for coming with his wife, Becky, to put me in and out of bed every day, help me dress, clean my room, cook all my meals, bring me to physical therapy three times a day, help me crutch over the ice, and tell me it was going to be okay when I couldn't stop crying.

To my editor, Julie Mustard—This book would not have happened without you. You took me and all my ideas, thoughts, and average writing skills and made something special out of it. You have a gift of giving things structure and helped me find my voice as a writer. Thank you for believing in me, having grace, and seeing this project through to the end.

Dean Blotto Gray, your photographs helped make this book unique; it is not just another book because of your genius. Thank you for documenting my snowboard career with creativity and excellence for the last eighteen years.

I spent a week in Switzerland for a shoot a few years back and only came away with one photo. Thank you, Mariell Vikkisk, for snapping that one shot on that dark and stormy night in Laax. It was all worth it, as it now adorns the cover of this book.

Shelly Tackett, your cover design made this book come to life; thank you.

Thank you, Gabe L'Heureux, for the portrait. I have loved shooting photos with you over the years, so I am glad to have one of your photos representing me well.

And Bobby Schwendenmann—you make things look good. You took my ideas and made them better. Thank you for doing the interior design, layout, and formatting. Your level of excellence is unmatched.

## BEYOND THE BOOK

To Lauren Loberg—Thank you for the years of support and friendship. I am pretty much a Jr. Sport Psychologist thanks to you. Many of the foundational life principles I learned from you are described throughout this book. Thank you for giving me the framework to work from and for always reminding me of who I really am.

To my longtime coach, Ricky Bower—Thank you for the last eleven years of coaching me. Your investment in me has helped me become the snowboarder I am today. Thanks for always holding me to a higher standard and for believing that I am still a spring chicken.

Thank you to my assistant, Natalie Mayer- You always look out for my best interests and have freely given me strength over and over again. Your belief in me is selfless, and I could not run my life or foundation without you.

Thank you to my good friends the Phillips—You guys have done life with me and helped me walk out some of the not-so-pretty seasons of change and growth. I am a healthier person thanks to your friendships. You always call greatness out of me and love me for who I am. Karen, thanks for always picking up the phone and praying with me.

Amanda Spuhler—I cannot count the number of times people have confused us for sisters. Thank you for your friendship; you truly are a sister to me. Thanks for encouraging me to sit down and write when I wanted to do yard work, play with the dog, or build things in the garage. Of course, thanks for kindly reminding me that there is a reason more people don't write books— because it's hard. Your steadiness and encouragement helped me see this project through to the end. You are more than anyone could ask for in a friend.

To the Lighthouse churches around the globe. Much of my growing up and personal development that I reference in this book was done with you. Thank you for the years spent; I will forever be thankful for that season of life.

To the worlds #1 preacher, Banning Liebscher, and my Jesus Culture Church family. Thanks for always championing me, for your prayers, and for challenging me to press in to God. Your community has sustained my snowboard career, allowed me to grow in my relationship with Jesus, and encouraged me to pursue my dreams like I never imagined.

# FOREWORD

Kelly is a source of inspiration for me, not every four years as the Olympics roll around, but every single day. I have countless inspiring memories of Kelly to share. But I want to begin with one that happened far away from halfpipes or podiums.

Two years ago, my husband spent several months in the ICU, paralyzed by a random autoimmune disease, hanging on to life by a thread. During this dark time in the ICU, I had to convince my husband that he would get better, because there were many times that he didn't believe he would. I also had to keep the faith and be positive for our three sons and the hundreds of employees at Burton Snowboards.

But there were moments when I was angry that he was going through this and wondered why it happened. For the most part, I kept these darker thoughts to myself, but Kelly was one of the few people I let in to share how truly grave the situation was and the depth of my own despair. Looking back, I think I instinctively turned to Kelly because she has a wisdom and inner strength beyond her years. She puts her beliefs—in love, in kindness and in faith—at the center of who she is. During my husband's illness, Kelly encouraged and inspired me to keep on believing that things would get better. And they did—my husband is fully recovered now.

To me, Kelly's strength during this difficult time was another validation of why she is a true champion both on and off the hill. As she herself acknowledges, Kelly is the definition of the "quiet champion"—humble and unassuming, yet driven to push the boundaries of her sport. Kelly's impact on the sport of snowboarding cannot be overstated. With three Olympic medals, over 75 wins, a 16-contest winning streak and more than 140 podium finishes, no other athlete—male or female—has accomplished more in the history of the sport, period.

In many ways, Kelly's story is the story of snowboarding—from obscurity to a mainstream Olympic showcase. When seven-year-old Kelly gave up her skis for a snowboard, there were no promises of fame or fortune, only a passion for the feeling of standing sideways.

Kelly went from good to great to completely unstoppable, dominating women's snowboarding for more than a decade. What was considered impossible became Kelly's "normal" as she pushed the edges of the sport by pushing her own personal limitations.

Just like Kelly was there for me during some of my happiest and darkest times, I have been fortunate to witness Kelly's extraordinary journey. Waiting anxiously and cheering loudly at the bottom of the pipe, I was there to celebrate her victories and help console her during setbacks.

One of the most unforgettable memories is of Kelly's run at the 2006 Winter Olympics in Torino. During the finals, I was standing at the bottom of the pipe and watched as Kelly put down the best run I had ever seen in women's snowboarding. What I couldn't see from where I was standing was that Kelly had lost her balance just a tiny bit after landing her last hit. So for a few moments, I was certain Kelly had won a second consecutive Olympic gold medal. Then I realized what happened and was heartbroken. Shortly after the competition, I talked to Kelly. And in true Kelly fashion, she cheered me up about her run. She said that a few years ago she would've been crushed. But now she was motivated by different things, and she was so proud that she had pushed women's snowboarding to a new level by ending her run with a huge 900—even if it resulted in a fall. She wouldn't let herself be defined by a medal. What mattered most was that she had progressed women's snowboarding.

Fast forward to 2011 at the Winter X Games in Aspen where Kelly sealed her win with her first run. Watching Kelly win gold at the X Games was nothing new. By 2011, Kelly had already clinched her 4th X Games gold when she stood at the top of the massive pipe to take her third and final run. We all knew she had a choice: take a well-deserved victory lap or attempt what we knew she had been working on: the trick called the frontside 1080 (three full rotations). If she landed it, she would be the first woman to ever land a 1080 in competition. Kelly, of course, chose the latter—making snowboarding history.

The moment that Kelly landed that 1080, I distinctly remember feeling like women's snowboarding was now in Kelly's hands, and we trusted her. And sure enough, once Kelly landed that trick, the impossible became possible in women's snowboarding all because she was driven to push herself and the sport instead of taking a victory lap.

Kelly's influence on snowboarding is unprecedented—not just because of her long list of victories and achievements, but also because of the victories and achievements she has inspired in others. Watch a press conference after a major competition and you'll hear how Kelly has inspired so many of her peers. Chloe Kim, who went on to make history in 2016 as the first female snowboarder to land back-to-back 1080s in competition, had this to say about Kelly in a recent *Denver Post* interview: "I've always looked up to Kelly's riding but especially her as a person. She is one of the most successful women snowboarders, and she is an amazing person. When I first met Kelly, she really took me under her wing and was really helpful."

As she shares in *Inspired*, the "secret" to her unprecedented leadership in snowboarding is the love she has for the people around her, the joy in what she does, and a deep self-confidence that comes from knowing how she defines success. "To know that I inspire people to be great and push themselves to the limits of what they are capable of, that's a huge success for me," said Kelly in a recent interview with CNN.

Now, in 2017, Kelly is going for her fifth Olympics. If she earns a spot on the highly competitive U.S. Women's Snowboard Team, she will make history yet again as the only snowboarder to ever compete in five Olympics. As much as I would love to support her again at the bottom of another Olympic halfpipe and see her with yet another medal around her neck, Kelly has already won in my mind. She has won because she has achieved what many athletes cannot: lasting happiness and success in the sport she loves. She has won because of her contributions to the sport. And she has won because she has inspired so many people both on and off the hill.


Donna Carpenter
Co-Founder/CEO, Burton

# INTRODUCTION

If you told me ten years ago that I would author a book, I would have called you crazy. To be honest, I struggled through high school academically mostly because I always put my athletics first. I guess that worked out for me, but throughout this process I have wished I had paid a little more attention in English class. Don't get me wrong; I am not unintelligent, but I don't learn well in the traditional sense of the word. In school, I struggled with reading and writing and was diagnosed with dyslexia when I entered seventh grade. From that point forward I remained in special education and received tutoring in almost all my classes to simply get a passing grade. How I think and understand things always seemed to be different than those around me, which I am finding out now is not always a bad thing.

After some success in my snowboarding career, I started receiving requests to "share my story." I got invited to businesses, schools, churches, companies, and leadership conferences to "inspire" them. In their eyes, I had achieved "success" and that success could be harnessed in a story that brought some sort of life or hope to people. I remember the first time I accepted one of the speaking invitations; I was scared and uncomfortable to share my story. In the beginning, I was so nervous. I just rushed through some facts and sat down not remembering what I even said and realizing that it probably didn't even make sense. We all have to start somewhere.

Even then, blundered storytelling and all, to my amazement, I kept receiving invitations. The more I spoke, the better I got. I noticed that I was not a natural when it came to public speaking, but as with anything else in life, the more you practice the better you get. It took me awhile to figure out who I am as a speaker. It was not about figuring out a format or how to be like someone else up on stage; it was about figuring out my own personal style. Now, after fifteen years of sharing my stories publicly, I am still nervous every single time. I guess it's a lot like snowboard contests in that way.

The more I developed as a speaker, the more I realized it was best to share on what I had to bring to the table that was unique to me. I did not have to be Miss Charismatic, the life of the party, a theologian, or present a 1, 2, 3 guide to life. I had to be me; that is what people wanted; they wanted to hear about me. I did not have to study about leadership or motivation or come up with some new revelation; I just had to be willing to let people in. Most people experience me through the persona I put out there. I am kind of quiet unless you know me; I am a Christian and an introvert. Those two things don't really make you popular in my industry or get you invitations to many places to inspire people.

One of the most significant speaking engagements was at a conference in New Mexico. As it was for some old friends who I loved and respected, I accepted the invitation and asked them to send me more information and details about the event as it became available. Later that week, I received a link to the website. As I scrolled through the information, I realized I was the main speaker for the weekend. I kept hoping I would find someone else, but it was just me. I thought to myself, *That can't be correct*, and then I looked at what musicians would be part of the event and I saw Kim Walker Smith's name. That was a name I knew; she had been to my church before, but I mostly knew of her because she was one of my favorite worship leaders.

It went from bad to worse. For any of you who are not familiar with Kim, she is one of the most influential, popular and straight-up biggest bosses in the Christian music world. Not only was I the main speaker, but also the other part of the event would be hosted by one of my heroes. The more I pondered it, the more I found myself trying to figure out if there was any way I could back out of this conference. Had it been pretty much anyone else who invited me, I just may have had the guts to cancel, but I could not bring myself to do it.

As I began to prepare for my sessions, all I felt was inadequate. What did I have that would measure up to this kind of requirement? What was I going to bring to the table and how could I even sit at the table with someone like Kim? As I revisited past talks, speeches and teachings, I kept coming back to the word *inspirational*. I wanted something revolutionary; I did not really need something that was just inspirational. I quickly discounted the word in my mind and kept digging into my computer files, desperately trying to come up with something that would measure up. To my frustration, I kept coming back to two simple words.

*Be inspirational.*

I kept thinking about how I would be perceived. Maybe people would just say, "We had an inspirational speaker," and to be honest, that seemed pretty lame to me. It would probably be the last time I got invited anywhere as the main speaker if I did that. Discouraged and frustrated, I grudgingly decided to explore what it meant to be inspirational.

As my Google searches started to pull up websites and articles, I found it intriguing. As I read, I saw that the first time the word *inspired* was used, people were using it to describe a supernatural being. As that related to my faith, I had a place for the supernatural. I was paying attention now. People did not know how to explain God; they did not have words for it, so they just said we are "inspired." The literal translation said that to be inspired meant "to breathe life into something."

I recounted the words in my head again, "I am to be inspirational." I thought, *How cool! I get to breathe life into people, into their dreams, into their lives.* I no longer thought it was cheesy and lame. I was beginning to see just what I was capable of doing. By putting my life on display, other people would be inspired in their own lives.

I went to New Mexico and did just that: I invited people in. I told them my stories and let them see how I think and how I work. I shared my mountain-top experiences with them and I also let them see me in the valleys of my life. At the end of it all, you know what they told me? They told me how inspiring I was; they told me that they were so *inspired*. With every conversation I had, I laughed to myself and took more ownership of my mission.

My mission is to *inspire*.

Whether I am overcoming a major obstacle in life, my nervousness around public speaking, or the learning disability that plagued my childhood, my mission is inspiration. It is the mission I set out to further and the heart behind this book. This book is not a how-to guide or a quick fix; rather, it will be fuel to the fire. My heart is that people would pursue their potential and be who they were created to be.

I speak from experiences, both from growing up and from learning who I am through snowboarding. If you know nothing about snowboarding, keep reading, because you will still relate to my stories. This book is for anyone who wants to grow and progress in life, individually or in their sport or career. I take snapshots and stories from all four of my Olympic trips, to illustrate principles and emphasize meaningful points. It does not follow a chronological timeline of my life, but I am including a timeline of my major life events as a reference for the stories I tell throughout the book.

If you need some new life breathed into you, if you need some courage and some inspiration, the pages of this book are an invitation for you to come in. Come enjoy these snapshots into my life, career, and process. As you read about my journey, I hope you are challenged and inspired to go on a journey of your own.

If nothing else, I hope you are truly *inspired*.

# TIMELINE

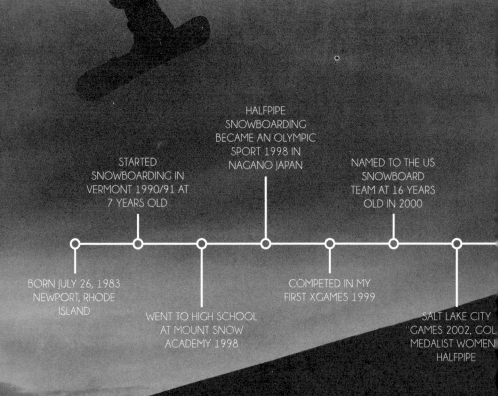

HALFPIPE
SNOWBOARDING
BECAME AN OLYMPIC
SPORT 1998 IN
NAGANO JAPAN

STARTED
SNOWBOARDING IN
VERMONT 1990/91 AT
7 YEARS OLD

NAMED TO THE US
SNOWBOARD
TEAM AT 16 YEARS
OLD IN 2000

BORN JULY 26, 1983
NEWPORT, RHODE
ISLAND

COMPETED IN MY
FIRST XGAMES 1999

WENT TO HIGH SCHOOL
AT MOUNT SNOW
ACADEMY 1998

SALT LAKE CITY
GAMES 2002, GOL
MEDALIST WOMEN
HALFPIPE

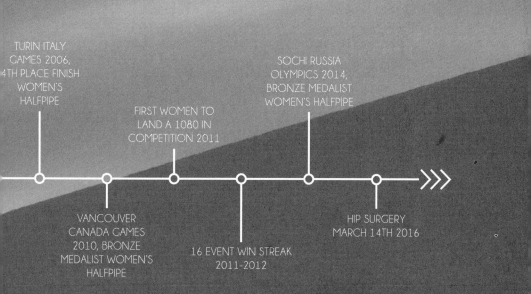

TURIN ITALY
GAMES 2006,
4TH PLACE FINISH
WOMEN'S
HALFPIPE

FIRST WOMEN TO
LAND A 1080 IN
COMPETITION 2011

SOCHI RUSSIA
OLYMPICS 2014,
BRONZE MEDALIST
WOMEN'S HALFPIPE

VANCOUVER
CANADA GAMES
2010, BRONZE
MEDALIST WOMEN'S
HALFPIPE

16 EVENT WIN STREAK
2011-2012

HIP SURGERY
MARCH 14TH 2016

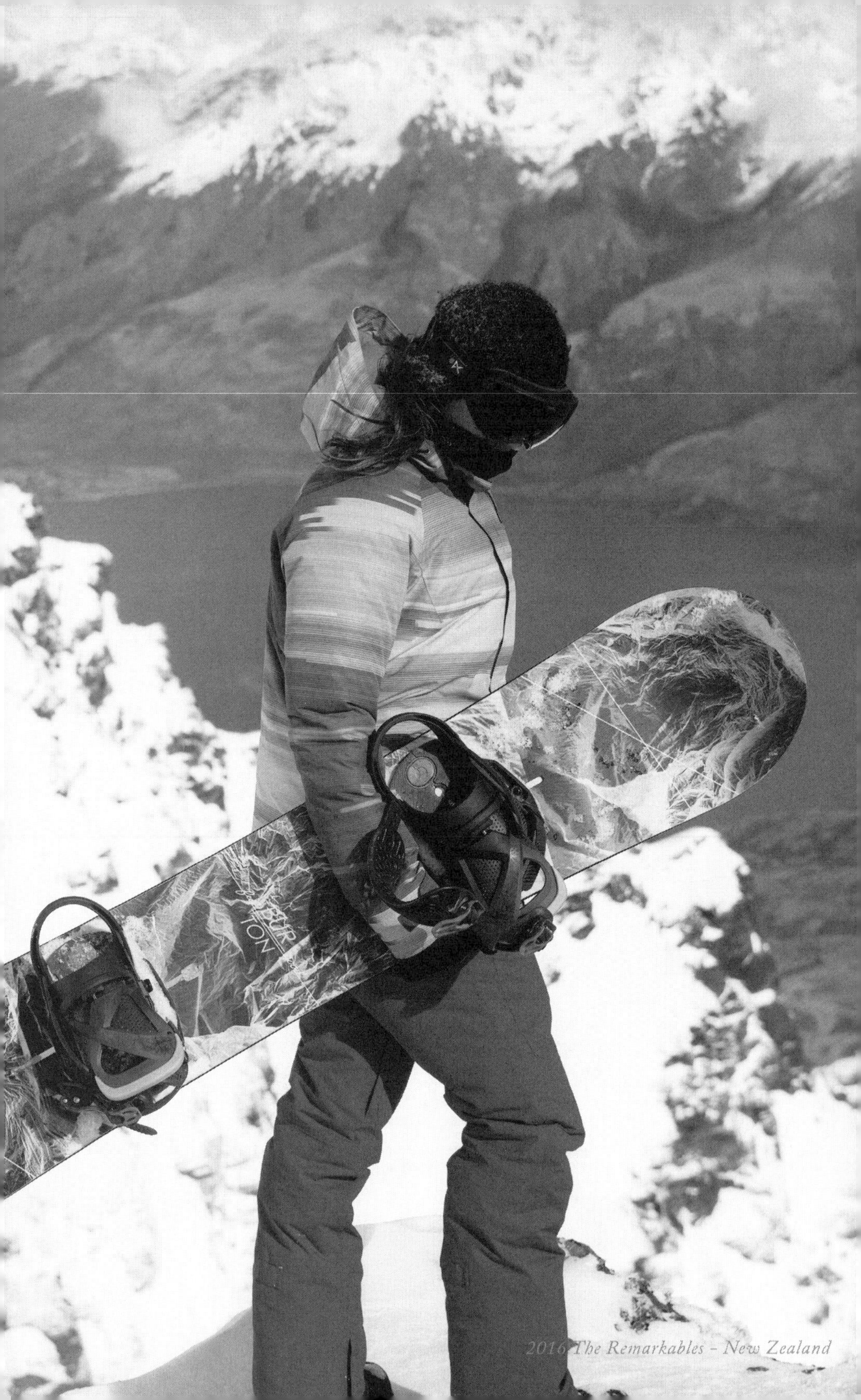


*2016 The Remarkables – New Zealand*

# CHAPTER ONE

# FROM THE TOP

*" When you grow up, you can be anything and do anything you want to. "*

*–My dad*

Thirty seconds is not a very long time. Considering there are over 86,000 seconds in one week, 32 million seconds in a year, and over 300 million seconds over the course of our lifetime, thirty seconds is nothing more than a blip on the line of eternity. My life revolves around increments of thirty seconds. I wait four years for my thirty seconds, to strap into my snowboard and see what I have built. How well I perform during this small snapshot of my life will determine my income, endorsements, and even my value in the eyes of the action sports world. Over the years, thirty-second intervals have encapsulated highs and lows, successes and failures. Through it all, I have found the one constant in my life is that nothing is constant.

## SNOWBOARDING: A LEGITIMATE OLYMPIC SPORT

The Winter Olympics were first held in 1924 with only a handful of the events we watch today. Snowboarding was definitely not one of them. In 1998, as a relatively new sport that was picking up momentum and gaining acceptance in the winter sport communities, snowboarding was first officially recognized at the Olympics in Nagano. A very rainy day and poor television coverage helped the snowboarding events go widely unrecognized at their debut.

As a fourteen-year-old, I didn't know I would be making decisions that would shape my life as I know it as I watched these Games unfold in 1998. I recorded the snowboard events on a VHS tape (if anyone remembers those). I sat and watched the Americans compete on that rainy day in Japan, wonder and possibility building in me, and I knew in that moment that this was what I wanted to do with my life. It was a defining moment for me, so I pointed my life in that direction and never looked back.

Over the next four years, events like the X Games helped push the sport into the living rooms of mainstream America, sparking interest from people who would otherwise be indifferent. By the Winter Olympics in 2002, expectancy for this new sport was brimming over. The airtime allotted on national television was exponentially increased from a mere forty minutes in Nagano to a staggering eight hours of coverage in Salt Lake City. The pressure was on.

In 2002, and each subsequent year, the snowboarding halfpipe competition began with the women's event followed by the men's runs the following day. If everything went according to plan, we started early in the morning and prepared for a long day. Just five months after the attack on the World Trade Center towers, security was beyond tight. After we had our vehicle checked for bombs and navigated through several metal detectors, we headed up to the halfpipe for the main event. Men greeted us with assault rifles around every lift and rope tow—not our normal scenario for a snowboard event. Add to that stadium seating that rimmed the bottom, and it was clear that an uncharacteristic event was in the making.

Unlike the events we see today that cater to progression and give opportunity to try new things, the format at that time was centered around constancy and a measured performance. There were twenty-three competitors from twelve different nations. With twelve girls making it to the finals, I needed to be on my game to ensure I had a spot in the main event. For years, I trained and prepared, knowing that one day I would find myself in that exact spot.

## MY ROAD TO 2002

In the sport of snowboarding, just because you are on the U.S. team doesn't mean you are guaranteed a spot on the Olympic team. It is the five events leading up to the games, the Grand Prix Olympic qualifiers, that decide who gets to go. This ensures that the United States sends the team with the best possible chance of medaling. There is a maximum of four spots per discipline, per country, per gender. The Federation of International Snowboarding (FIS) list from the year before would determine if we would be able to use all four allotted spots for that year. There were four men from America seeded but the women only had three spots to fill. This meant that after the five qualifying Grand Prix events, only the top three American women would go on to represent the United States at the Olympics. In 2002, this was not good news for me.

*"It is not so much what happens that interests me, rather how I respond in these moments that show me what I am made of."*

I had a very difficult year. When I look at the hardships that play out in my day-to-day life, they can appear catastrophic and, at times, earth shattering. In hindsight, they can appear trivial at times too. It is not so much what happens that interests me, rather how I respond in these moments that show me what I am made of. I struggled through most of the qualifiers.

The Grand Prix events were far from a cakewalk. My parents came out to support me in my first two Olympic Qualifiers in Mammoth, California. I had never experienced pressure like that before. In short, I choked. I choked bad. It was amplified by the fact that my family had flown 3,000 miles to watch their girl make something of herself. After all, I was deferring college to make snowboarding my career and this would make or break it for my father. It was looking like I was leaning way more towards breaking it than making it at this point.

I was heartbroken. In my mind, I had five opportunities, which seemed like a lot. If you added up all the thirty second runs, I had at least ten whole minutes of my life to make my dream come true, and I only needed one minute to make it count. It was still possible. Now, I was down to only six minutes left. Instead of adding insult to injury, I added injury to my broken morale.

We were skipping Christmas with our families that year to get in more training. Since I did not have any victories to speak of, I thought it was in my best interest to get more practice. It was a snowy day in Mammoth and I was hammering my body, trying desperately to land the trick I had fallen on in every run of the qualifiers thus far. It was a simple McTwist (front flip 540) and I was finally getting it. I was landing it almost perfectly until I took it too deep and felt a stab of pain in my knee—it looked like I would make it home for Christmas after all. I took a quick trip to Utah for an MRI, which showed that I had torn my lateral meniscus.

I had a tough call to make—try to baby it, control the swelling, stop practicing so much and give the qualifiers a shot, or go and get it fixed now. At that point, I did not have much to lose. A few more events, six minutes to be exact, and my Olympic dreams would be over anyway. If I could deal with the pain and not aggravate it, then I would give it a go. After all, it would be four more years before I had another chance at the Games.

After much deliberation, I went with the no practice plan. As I entered the third qualifier at Mount Bachelor, Oregon, I was told that I had only ten runs allotted to me each day; this was what the physical trainer felt comfortable letting me do. Normally, I would do close to twenty runs. Theoretically, I would be able to get used to the pipe while not making my knee look like a balloon or injuring it any further. Sounded like a great plan at the time.

> *"Sometimes when we let go of our dreams we, in turn, let go of any expectation that is attached to them."*

As much as I didn't want to admit it, by this point, I waved goodbye to my dream. Goodbye to a dream that I had dreamt since I watched that VHS recording of Nagano after school. I didn't relegate my career as finished, but I came to terms with my first Olympics probably happening four years down the road. I counted my chances of making the team one last time; I already failed in the first two events. I choked mentally, and now my youthful ambition and health were gone too. I believed there was nothing I could do to make this better. Sometimes when we let go of our dreams we, in turn, let go of any expectation that is attached to them, and perhaps in that moment, letting go is just what I needed to do.

Ten runs a day is not a lot, especially when I did not have any time to spare. I was going to have to make each run count, so I came up with a plan. I would start by getting the first and second runs out of the way, move into my tricks, and by run five I would be in full swing. Much to my surprise, not only did I find those first few runs tolerable for my knee, but I was also riding better than before. Plus, I was landing the trick that I had not been able to in Mammoth: the McTwist. I was doing it. I was actually doing the run that I knew would land me on the podium.

Sometimes tricks come and go, but this one had finally come and it came to stay. I was calling it my own, and I was landing it every time. As the third qualifier came to an end, I found myself in yet another new position. I had a 7th, a 9th, and now a 1st place win. With two events left and one good placing, my hope was back, my dream raised from the dead, and I was still in the race. Even though I still had a daily limit of runs, I knew it was enough.

Heading into the next two qualifiers, I took what I had learned and went full steam ahead. I learned the valuable lesson of how detrimental external pressures can be. It was, and is still, a lesson that is always evolving and revealing more of itself to me. But because I had seen the tip of the iceberg, I was able to navigate around it. I saw very simply how easy it is to allow outside pressures shape my reality. If I could keep the idea that I had nothing to lose and it did not matter how I did, I could keep performing well. I would not say that is a good goal to have as an approach—not very sustainable—but it would do the trick for me in that season. I went and fought for that mental space and came out on top of the next Olympic qualifier. I had done it; I was going to the Olympics.

Up until this point I had only been competing against other people from the United States. I was yet to see how I would stack up against the rest of the world. America is notorious for having some of the best riders in the world, but it is a big world and Norway, Canada, and Germany were sure to have some serious contenders. The next event would be a great opportunity to see how my best run, which had won the last three events, would hold up against the rest of the world. With this, I entered the biggest event of our sport in any non-Olympic year—the X Games.

Again, I found feet solid underneath me, which is always in your best interest in the sport of snowboarding. My knee was still holding its own.

Less than three weeks out from the Olympic Games and I knew I had what it takes to go up against the people who I have looked up to my entire snowboarding career. I won these X Games, and not by just a few points. I was twelve points ahead of the rest of the field. I left there with the shocking realization that if I landed on my feet I had the potential to beat the rest of the world, and perhaps be the best in the world. My, how the tides turned.

In two short months, I went from being a train wreck, to wrecking my body, to heartbreak, to having hope, and now seeing that my hope was rightly placed because I had the results to prove that I could achieve what I was setting out to do. I was the youngest member of the United States Halfpipe Team. I would be representing my country on home soil, and, if I played my cards right, I could just maybe end up with the dream of all dreams—an Olympic medal.

I could not go there. I could not let that expectation get to me. I could not allow myself to think like that or say that I had hopes of winning. I had to stick with what I knew to work. It did not matter how I did; there could be no expectation. After all, everything was a gift at this point, right? I had nothing and I must keep that attitude to keep the good performances coming in. It was not an approach that would help me be my best; it allowed me to survive in the moment. I was still going to try to advance, but it was more about self-preservation than a personal best performance. I had made the team; now I could set my next little step out there—I would try to medal. I would survive and medal.

## SALT LAKE CITY OLYMPICS

The pressure of life being divided into seconds is different from the typical pressure an eighteen-year-old faces. Normal teenagers struggle with things like wanting to be liked, passing their driving test, and hoping to have a date to the prom. I, however, was barely out of high school and living the biggest moment of my young life—leading my peers into the finals of the Olympic Games in Salt Lake City. Only in my wildest dreams had I imagined being there. Instead of saying yes to the prom dress, I was standing atop the most daunting halfpipe I'd faced in my young life.

---

*"It is a fine line between elation and heartache in the world of competitive sports."*

---

As one of the youngest competitors in the event, I watched some of my heroes go before me and land spots in the finals. I also watched some of the former medalists and favorites go down—their Olympic dreams coming to an end. Some of them were never heard from or seen again, their competitive career's ending that day. It is a fine line between elation and heartache in the world of competitive sports. I knew at this point there was nothing else I could acquire that would help me on this day. My preparation is all I would have to get me through.

I felt out of place surrounded by experienced athletes and seasoned competitors on every side. If that wasn't enough, there were 17,000 spectators surrounding the halfpipe who came out just to cheer us on. To top it all off, my country was hosting these Olympic Games, the Games where I would be making my first Olympic appearance. To say I was nervous was an understatement. The Olympic flame had been lit for two days; my nerves were revved up and my time had come. I was "dropping in" next.

I had done this many times before. I always say, "I started snowboarding before it was cool." It started for me in 1990, the year when snowboarding was first allowed at my home hill, Mount Snow, Vermont. (This was one of the first resorts on the east coast that purchased a halfpipe-grooming machine called a "Pipe Dragon.") At ten years old, I began to ride through the halfpipe. Shortly after, I discovered how much I loved it. I would spend hours enjoying the daily challenges it presented to me, even the grudging hikes up the hill. It quickly became more than a hobby; it was my passion.

I knew I was dropping into a thirty second window that would be a deciding factor for me, possibly defining my future. I did my first run and, to my honest surprise and excitement, I found myself on my feet having "put down" the run I had hoped for, and was sitting in first place. I not only was going to the finals, but I was the first seed! It was strange to see my dream become a reality after all those years.

Now these Olympics were unlike any other event I had ever seen in snowboarding. Unlike any sporting event I had ever been to, we had uniforms, things to wear to opening ceremonies, and we were even given specific clothes to wear to bed. We had credentials, things we should say and things we should not say. I had never experienced anything like it. It was a whirlwind of nerves and expectations. Standing on the hill that day, all I could think about was how little time I had left—sixty seconds to be exact.

I had sixty seconds left to prove myself. I could do that. I could survive sixty more seconds and perhaps, just maybe, I could walk away with something to show for it. But I couldn't allow myself to think that way. I was in survival mode and decided I had no need to get ahead of myself. I did not need to think about the outcome; I needed to focus on the present. Two runs and this crescendo would be over. Okay, one run at a time: thirty seconds and then thirty more.

This event, I would drop last as I was the number one qualifier. It would be all up to me to land my run. As competitors dropped in and completed their runs, I thought, *Perhaps people were holding back; perhaps I have not seen their best?* No, I refused to go there. I had to do what I came there to do—my run. My run that I call my own. Would it be enough?

There were no surprises; everyone was right where I thought they would be, doing exactly what I thought they were capable of doing. Much to my surprise, I did exactly what I wanted to do. I did my run just as I had done the last four events. Deafened by the cheers of 17,000 of my new friends, I stood there in awe, staring at the points board and wondering if I was going to do it, wondering if I was going to walk away with something to show for all my efforts. I was thinking that I had done what I came there to do—I had won a medal.

One run was over, should I now dare to dream again? Still, I had nothing to lose. Sure, I would go for it and maybe win the gold medal.

I watched some of my friends land the runs we all hoped they would— Kjersti Buaas sending a huge Air to Fakie and seeing Tricia Byrnes land the elusive McTwist, both in their final runs, was astounding to watch. Those runs landed them each in a respectable 4th and 6th place. I was sitting in second place as it came around to my final run in finals. Dorian Vidal of France landed her 720, and it was just enough to bump me to that second-place position. I still had the good seeding, which left me to be the last one to drop. Now, quite literally, I had nothing to lose. I would give it my all and was going to medal no matter what happened.

Headphones turned up as loud as they could go were not enough to drown out the cheers. I would go across the flat bottom of the halfpipe and be able to hear Blink 182 in my headphones, while everything above the lip of the wall was people screaming. This was it—one chance.

You can't write scenarios like this. It was my first Olympics, home country, last run, and I already had a silver medal. I was pulling out all the stops. I went for it. I went bigger and faster than I had ever gone, just barely keeping my adrenalin in check. Every hit was exactly as I had planned all the way till my last two hits, which would be the most technical: McTwist and Frontside 720—done and done.

Hands raised, I knew I had done it. I looked to my coach in the finish area and shrugged my shoulders in astonishment. Now I just had to wait for the scores to come in. I scored 47.9 out of 50, which might as well have been perfect. In just thirty seconds, I had won the Olympic Games.

## GROWING UP FAST

Small town girl to Olympic gold medalist: it does happen. You will never know all the things that go along with winning the first gold medal at your country's Olympics until you are thrust into it. If I said my schedule was busy, that would be an understatement. I went from being a nobody to being America's golden girl. I think I lived in a state of shock.

There were sixteen days of Olympic competition during which I traveled in and out of the airport eleven times. There was not much time for rest those first few days. On day three post event, I remember my agent coming to my house and literally pulling me out of bed and force-feeding me coffee. If I remember correctly, there were protests and tears of exhaustion involved. Before 2002, I had never had my makeup or hair done. Now I was having my face painted two to three times a day in order to be presentable for the next event I was booked to attend. My eyes were so tired that when I would shut them to put on makeup, they would fill with tears almost uncontrollably.

*"My life felt like a sleepless dream for a good year or two."*

From the moment in the medals plaza when I watched my flag rise and heard the national anthem of the United States of America play, I was on the go. There was no going home the night I won, as the boys had their event the next day; we were banned from the team house. My life felt like a sleepless dream for a good year or two.

I kept up with snowboarding; it was actually a refuge. I remember jumping at the chance to go to Japan with my team the day after closing ceremonies so I could catch up on sleep at last. It was short-lived. I headed back from Japan to finish out the rest of my competitive season, ending it by winning my first U.S. Open—a hallmark of my career and the perfect end to the season of my dreams. The media attention would continue: interviews with Dave Chappelle on Leno, *The Late Show with David Letterman*, from teaching Katie Couric to snowboard, to attending the Daytona 500 race from the pits, hanging with Britney Spears (and, yes, Justin Timberlake as they were dating at the time) in New York, getting calls from Blink 182, ringing the opening bell at the New York Stock exchange, being in multiple parades, as well as a White House visit—just to name a few of the things that were in the mix.

Talk about a change in pace. I never dreamed beyond winning. I was so focused on the task at hand and surviving that I did not even consider what things would be like if I actually made it. I define what I had done by saying, "I made it." Not many people ever get to say that, much less when they are eighteen years old. It was a strange and unfamiliar place. Don't get me wrong; I was very proud of what I had accomplished. It is just that in less than thirty seconds, my life went from being predictable and normal to a completely different reality. No one can prepare you for such a drastic change.

This change began one of the craziest roller coasters of the life I call mine. It has taken me all over the world to compete, to speak, to inspire, and leads me into self-reflection and continual pursuit of progress.

## REFLECTION QUESTIONS

*What does your "30 seconds" look like?*

*How did past decisions shape your life significantly?*

*What are you hoping for in your life?*

# CHAPTER TWO
# FINDING YOUR WHY

*"The two most important days in your life are the day you were born and the day you find out why."*

*–Mark Twain*

Every four years the gold medal favorites and the dark horses line up to make the U.S. Olympic team—the would-bes and the has-beens, the most talented athletes and the brightest rising stars, all together fighting for the same dream. Four years is a long time; I have navigated that time and space many times as I am now looking to my fifth Olympics. A lull exists between the four-year cycle of Olympic snowboarding. People look to the "big show" but often forget the in-between day-to-day training it takes to get there. It is not for the unmotivated; I have seen many people come and go in my career because some are not able to stay motivated in the in-betweens.

The Olympics are the pinnacle of athletic achievement. They represent so much more than tradition or routine; the Games have the ability to transcend individual sports, culture, and even time. Winning on this stage is the universal image of greatness and achievement, but what does "greatness" and "winning" mean to those of us who have given everything to get it?

I think that is a great question; it isn't meant to be rhetorical. Many athletes finish the Olympic games and find themselves asking that very question: Why? Why did I just put myself through that? Why am I doing this? Why have I chosen this path? Unfortunately, many people don't stop to think about the why. Without a why, there is very little motivating you to get out of bed, put in the work, and go after all those big dreams. Don't get me wrong; I am a firm believer in dreaming big and going after it; my life is a testament to that. But finding your why is the single most important aspect of a successful and meaningful career. Why? Because everything starts at why.

## WITHOUT A WHY THERE IS NO HOW

In elementary school, students are taught the elements of a story: who, what, when, why, and how. In the current story of my life, the first few blanks seem simple to fill in:

Who? Kelly Clark

What? Professional snowboarder

When? 2016 looking to the 2018 Winter Olympic Games

Why? Because I love the sport and want to leave a legacy

How? Overcome the odds and work harder than ever before

Even these first few blanks are determined by story elements that come after: the why and the how. If I change my why, everything else changes, including the how. Without my why, I can only have a how for a very short amount of time. That short amount of time is probably not going to be sustainable, much less fun. Why? Because without a motivating reason for why we are doing something, we quickly find ourselves in survival mode. Instead of thriving, having fun, and looking forward to the thrill of competition, we end up trying to just survive this dream. Looking back, that is much of how I operated at my first Olympic games.

> *"It's in the in-between when we
> need to know our why the most."*

You could argue that my why should be obvious. I mean, it's the Olympics and snowboarding: two of the greatest things on this planet. I would argue back, however, that the obvious answer is usually not the correct one. I cannot have my why simply be an event that happens every four years; I need to know the why in the in-between because if I don't, then I have four years of wasted time. It's in the in-between when we need to know our why the most.

## ENCOUNTERING AN "OLD" FRIEND

It was a quite early morning; I stood at the top of the halfpipe alone. It was just over two years since the last Olympics, the halfway point until the next Games in Korea. In the spring, people come up a bit later in the day, so snow softens with the sun and is more forgiving for learning new tricks. I often go up early as I have to get warmed up; it takes a little more time for me as I am twice as old as some of my competitors. I like doing this ritual in the quiet, alone.

It turns out on this morning, I was not alone. I heard the loud scraping sound on the frozen slush behind me, and to my surprise, an old friend joined me on the hill. We are old in the sense that most competitors are half our age. The two of us shared the spotlight together in a few Olympics, but I hadn't seen her in ages.

After not seeing much of her for a few years, I found it strange that she showed up early on this firm morning to "train" in the halfpipe—perhaps she thought the same of me. We looked at each other with the same question running through our minds: What am I doing up so early training? We were two of the most successful athletes in our sport with the Olympics still almost two years out—no coaches, no teammates, just us. What were we doing there before anyone showed up? That is the very question we asked each other.

In a sport that is stereotyped as extreme and full of adrenaline junkies, we don't always talk about the behind-the-scenes aspects of our training. It is not glamorous or very marketable, but it is the foundation of our sport. Let's be real: no one wants to see me spending extra time every morning warming up or see the hours I spend every night recovering so I can go put on a good show the next day at the event. We, as athletes, don't often put it on display or talk about what it takes. Our conversations to each other rarely extend beyond Instagram posts and what show we are binge watching on Netflix.

After I got done joking around about how long it took to get my body going in the morning, I asked her what she was doing. It is not a normal thing to have deep conversations at the top of the pipe. This morning was different; there were no crowds or cameras, no fans asking for autographs. All the fanfare and hype were gone and I found my friend looking for motivation; she was trying to fall in love with snowboarding again.

She talked about other things she was passionate about, identifying why she loved them. She then went into mistakes she made in the past, the ones that haunted her in quiet moments. Looking at past snowboarding events, she highlighted poor decisions and explained why she had failed. She even drew the conclusion that it was beneficial for her to fail because it taught her how not to fail again—all valid points. To be honest, it was a very mature way to look at things.

I jumped in where I could relate and expressed understanding. I was hearing much of my own journey in her process. I certainly had been there and was no stranger to the feeling of carrying the weight of the world on my back. Trying to have a sense of security and identity, I too had performed to prove to people who I was. I knew the heartache of coming up short, of not living up to the expectation of others, and failing to meet the extreme expectation I put on myself. Attempting to sustain something beyond a moment of glory? Yes, that too. Perhaps I was one of few people in the world who could relate, but I resonated with every word coming out of her mouth.

She must have realized that I was in the boat with her. Sometimes you relate because you have the same career, beliefs, or experiences, but it is not too often you find a few of those things that overlap. When they do, as in this moment, it makes you stop. She was realizing, just as I did, that we were on a similar journey, that on this early morning I may hold a key she was searching to find.

She stopped and looked at me for a long time before asking me a three-word question: "What motivates you?" After all, I was in the 16th year of the same journey she was on. If I were to do some reflecting, I would find many of the same successes and failures, victories and regrets. Four Olympic games, a bunch of medals, and a whole heap of losses. I might have won and lost just about every snowboarding event in the history of the sport. She was now asking me why. Why are you here early in the morning? Why are you here before anyone is up? The Olympics are not for another two years and you have been there many times before: "Why are you still here?" she asked me, because that was the very question she was asking herself.

> *"I have something left to give, something to contribute to snowboarding."*

I looked back at her knowing that what I had to say may not be what she wanted to hear. It was not going to be a quick fix. A "do this and you will win everything, you will always be happy, and money will fall from the sky" kind of solution was not to be found. Instead, I answered her in the only way I knew how, and the only way a friend like her deserved.

I answered her honestly: "I have something left to give, something to contribute to snowboarding."

Stunned, she replied, "Really? That's what motivates you? I have never thought of it like that. I don't know how to think of it like that."

## NEXT

After every Olympics, before I can even get out of my boots, it seems as though I answer the "What's next?" question countless times. After the Sochi Olympics, I got a new set of questions about my durability in addition to my future: "Are you finally done?" Some were gentler, like, "What else is there left for you do to?" As always, I have my preplanned quotes and polished media answers ready to go. I am quite good at speaking in sound bites for these impromptu inquiries; it is one of my special gifts. As I replied to these questions over and over again, I started to think about the questions with a bit more reflection. Eventually, I started to ask myself those hard questions in order to find an answer beyond, "I'll stop when I stop having fun," or as Tom Brady puts it, "When I suck, I'll retire."

It is easy to make your motivation about your destination. Though they are essentially connected, your destination or end goal cannot be your only motivator. You cannot get to the destination by only focusing on the destination. If we don't learn to embrace the journey, we will not get to enjoy our chosen destination, even if we make it there. We will just survive long enough to call it good and done and then step back and wonder why we put ourselves through that process. The journey is the process and the process is the journey.

## THE AMERICAN DREAMERS

As an American, I am a dreamer. I didn't realize until I traveled the world and met people from all different cultures that dreaming is not that common. The American dream is a real thing—to Americans. It is an amazing part of our heritage and our culture. This truly is the land of opportunity—where kids are not only asked what they want to do, but they are told they can actually do it. It may be our normal here in America, but it is far from normal.

It is truly a wonderful, unique thing to be inspired and believed in. The problem with this American mentality is that it can make us egocentric. With this type of ambition, things can become narrow, we get tunnel vision, and pretty soon we become the only ones who matter. We are some of the best dreamers, but a byproduct of that type of thinking is that we are very self-focused. As an athlete, this gets magnified greatly. We are basically programmed to think about ourselves; it is in the fine print of our job requirement.

The issues come when you spend all that time and energy on yourself and put it all into your own dreams. If you operate that way, the dream will live and die with you. We need to be dreamers who think bigger than ourselves. We need to be people who think that our dream is important, but we also need to think about how our dream could benefit others. Do I want to get to the end of my snowboarding career and realize that I only left behind good competition results? Will I find that I spent almost 20 years of my life on something to have a few records and medals to show for it? That would be sobering.

*"Our belief system shows up in what we do, how we act, and how we respond to change."*

## CHANGING MY LENS

Motivation has a lot to do with the lens through which we look. Charles Swindoll famously said, "Life is 10 percent what happens to you and

90 percent what you do with it." Your actions actually show you what you think; they are directly related. Our belief system shows up in what we do, how we act, and how we respond to change. If you want to change the way you act, you have to first adjust the way you think. It is our perspective or the lens that we look through that matters. What you believe to be true is displayed in your actions and behaviors. If you have some healthy, stable values established in your life, then you will have stability and a steady lens that you look through. You will have something to pull on, something to guide you, non-negotiables in your life that help you through anything life can throw at you. Your principles cannot be malleable and change based off what is going on around you. Rather, they are independent and the backbone of your day-to-day actions regardless of what is going on around you. If the way you view the world is not lined up with good principles, then the principles are not helpful and won't produce beneficial things in your life.

As you grow, your lens can change, and as it changes, it actually matures if you're willing to take feedback. A few years ago, through a series of events in my life, I came to the conclusion that I was looking to others—other people, organizations, companies, and even the snowboard industry—to give me things. I was always asking myself what I could get out of this. You may be saying to yourself, "Kelly, that's normal." Yes, I think it is a normal lens to look through. The problem is, however, that it was very unfulfilling because it was very need-based. When things are need-based, they set you up to have life happen to you instead of you participating intentionally in it. It is not a very influential way to live. Living to get your needs met creates a lot of instability and heartache through the avenue of disappointment. Believe it or not, we are not meant to be sustained by what goes on around us, rather what goes on in us.

I realized I wanted to change my outlook on life, and I decided I would change my lens. Instead of asking myself what I could get, I started asking myself what I could give. This would not be easy; it takes healthy boundaries, a fair amount of stamina, and courage to do this. By making this choice, I no longer allow myself to adjust my actions to get needs met. This is not an outlook resulting in short-term personal gain, but I have found it to be a much more fulfilling and sustainable lens to look through.

I applied this new lens to my snowboarding. When I was asked why I was still competing after 16 years, what was I there to get, I saw things a little differently. It was a small adjustment that brought a clear focus. When I began to think about what I could contribute to snowboarding,

> *"In reality, if I was here to get something,
> I should have stopped a long time ago."*

so many things became possible that weren't even in my field of view previously. My new lens made things much clearer. In reality, if I was here to get something, I should have stopped a long time ago. I have been to four Olympics and sixteen X Games; if I was here to get something, I already possessed it. I don't think I would be very motivated after all this time to keep pursuing things I already had. Asking myself, "What can I give?" keeps me motivated.

## WHAT LENS ARE YOU LOOKING THROUGH?

It is still okay to go after your goals. Even at this point in my career with the lens that looks at others as well as myself, I still have goals. When I look at contributing and investing in others, it does not mean that my personal goals are no longer important or don't matter; rather, they are viewed and supported by a diverse outlook. My goals have multiplied and work in tandem supporting each other. Yes, I push myself to win the events, but I also count my day a success when I am able to encourage the girls around me. I still have the same approach, but I am just not the center anymore, and my definition of success has broadened. This new perspective diversifies my investment in this industry I love so much. The calculation is simple: If I hit my potential, then I know the sport will benefit.

At this point, I am not sure I have hit my potential. I know I have something left to give to the industry, so I am motivated to keep going no matter how many years pass or how young my competitors are. In a way, thinking like this protects my almost twenty-year investment. I will go after the tricks and the wins on contest days, but I will get up in the morning thinking that I have an incredible opportunity to contribute to the sport, the companies I represent, and to the people I interact with daily. The simple act of writing this book is an extension of this approach: I want my life to contribute to people that I may never meet; perhaps you will hear my journey and be encouraged to continue after your own growth and goals.

> *"The calculation is simple: If I hit my potential, then I know the sport will benefit."*

One of the biggest roadblocks people have when adjusting their perspective to being motivated by what goes on inside us rather than by external measures is the lack of attention or fame attached to it. While it is not sustainable or enjoyable to be motivated by external things, it can be exhilarating at times. Because when it does work out, when you do win big, everyone sees it. You are the center of attention. Unfortunately, the risk is not worth the reward 95 percent of the time. I know all about calculating risk and reward and have found it disappointing almost every time. Achievement and so-called fame as a result of it always fade. They fade quicker than we would like to admit, especially in the information age that we live in where the next headline is only a scroll and click away. The real stinger lies in our own perspective of events. If you choose to be motivated by external things and become addicted to the attention it brings when it happens to work out, your own contentment and outlook of yourself will fade with the fame. When it does, hopelessness and depression will often land close to people who depend on external things to fulfill them. This is a powerless place to live. You will constantly be at the mercy of things you cannot control and constantly look to your circumstances to lift you up; and when they can't lift you up, it's easy to play the blame game.

What if I was at an event and I prepared well and I had a dream run in my mind. I knew what I wanted to do and I actually went out there and did it well; I even did it perfectly. I wasn't alone. Someone else, or three someone elses, did what they came to do and did it better than me. Therefore, I end up off the podium and discouraged. If I was motivated by external success, I would not be able to celebrate my personal success that I had that day. It would be easy for me to look at the results and say, "Well, I really blew it." The reality is that you knew what you wanted to do and you came out and did it, and that is a win. Not everyone will see it that way, but you have to make sure your heart sees it that way or you will begin the shift into setting yourself up to be successful only when it looks like you do what everyone else is doing. I can tell you from experience—that is not sustainable or fun.

## A NEW YEAR

I went into the 2014 Olympics as the gold medal favorite. From 2010-2014 I had won 86 percent of the events I entered. My consistency was staggering for anyone, let along someone in their late 20s. I had spent years shaping my skills, but these four years were more about shaping my outlook. I knew what I wanted to do. People think that it is an easy thing to put a snowboard run together. It is far from that. I knew what I was working toward as far as tricks for two years before the games. My coaches knew and my whole support team worked toward that one goal—the perfect run when it counts most. It is one thing to have the skill set, and it is another thing to execute it.

We knew that the Sochi venue had the potential to have variable snow conditions as we had experienced that one year out at the test event. The weather was warm and the snow was soft, creating inconsistency in the pipe. Nonetheless, I was determined to not let my circumstances dictate what kind of choices I made. I was determined to do my run no matter how bumpy and scary the halfpipe was. At the test event, I overcame some wild runs and put down a run good enough for the win that day. I knew if I wanted to be standing on the podium one year later, I would have to practice in every sketchy, bumpy pipe to be ready for whatever snow conditions I came up against.

*"I would not let my circumstances be responsible for my actions. I was going to be me in the midst of it all."*

When we arrived in Sochi we knew it was going to be bad, but we did not know that it would be this bad. The pipe was almost unrideable. You want the Olympics to be the most progressive pinnacle event of your sport, and it looked like this was going to be more about survival than progression. Still I was steadfast in my approach; I was not going to blame the pipe or the conditions. I decided ahead of time that after the event, I would not talk to the media and say the pipe condition was a contributing factor to our level of competition. I would not let my circumstances be responsible for my actions. I was going to be me in the midst of it all. I was one of the only women to try her full contest run before the day of the event. We usually get 4-5 days of practice, but the pipe was so poorly built that many deemed it unsafe to practice in and they chose to save the pipe for the event. We practiced only a handful of those scheduled days in short time frames as the pipe would deteriorate quickly.

I still thought I could do it. I had done everything in my ability to prepare well. I came out in qualifiers and placed second after the first run, but

I wanted that top qualifier spot. So, I went for it and put down the top qualifying run of the day with my second attempt. The run finals are in reverse qualifying order and I had that last start position. Therefore, I would go into the last run of the event knowing what I needed to do to win.

I then waited almost six hours for the finals to start. Three rounds of competition had happened in the pipe that day and when we showed up for finals it had severely deteriorated. The halfpipe was literally tilted sideways and melting out with large bumps in the transition. This becomes very difficult for us as we are heading full speed at a stationary wall and if that wall has bumps or holes it becomes like a speed bump or a pothole. Those are hard to navigate at slow speeds, and even more difficult when you are traveling full speed trying to do your biggest trick in an Olympic final. I was determined to go for it: I could not let my circumstances decide what kind of run I would do. After all it was the Olympics and I had been waiting four years for my thirty second window.

The practice before the final usually sets the tone of your final runs and that night I fell five of five practice runs. I moved my 1080 four times to get it to work somewhere in that pipe. Being adaptable is good. It's like taking a detour; you will arrive at the same destination, but how you get there may look a little different than anticipated. I was still trying to make it happen that night and as practice wound down I was yet to land a run. I went to the bottom of the pipe and I saw a sea of friends and U.S. team staffers. They were all looking at me blankly, knowing that my night was going about as wrong as it could go. I pulled my sports psych aside and said, "You know what I need? I need a good cry." So, we went around the back of the stadium seats and I cried for about 30 seconds. Not just watery eyes and sniffles, but a cry that I like to call the "ugly cry," the kind that causes you not to be able to breathe or see. After that I declared that I was ready to go. It's okay to get disappointed along the way, you just can't stay there. There is a saying I like: "If you are going through hell, keep going." I was ready to keep going.

Even though it looked impossible, it still was an opportunity. It was my 30 seconds and I was going to make it happen instead of giving up. I then proceeded to fall in my first run in epic fashion. I "hit the deck" and then did a backflip off the 22ft wall to the flat bottom where I tacoed. Even if you don't know much about snowboarding, you should be able to visualize that scene. Oddly enough, I was more prepared for a first run fall than I was for the bad practice. It was what I had practiced more during my in-between. I had been preparing for the worst-case scenario so I could rise above if needed. Sure, enough, I was looking at this as an opportunity to overcome. I went to the top and that was the first thing I said to my coaches: "What an opportunity! Good thing I got ready for this." I knew what I came here to do regardless of what was going on around me. These were my 30 seconds and nothing was going to get in the way of that.

> *"It's okay to get disappointed along the way; you just can't stay there."*

I write this as if it were all principles and preparation and somehow glamorous. The reality is that on this side of the victory, things seem more glamorous and less scary. I think that is always the case when looking back on impossible situations that worked out. I can honestly say that the next run was singlehandedly the most difficult thing I have ever done. I had the chance to make it happen or lose it all in just one run. I was the last person to go of the entire event. The podium was set, apart from one last run by me, the gold medal favorite, the person who had won 86 percent of the events she had entered over the last four years, the one who also had not landed a run in her last six attempts, and the girl who was "ugly crying" not too long ago.

In short, I landed. I made it through the run. I can't begin to tell you the relief and exhilaration that I experienced. It was not my best snowboarding, but it was the run that I went there to do. I did not back down, play it safe or leave there with regrets. It was one of my greatest victories, not because I earned an Olympic bronze medal but because of what I personally overcame that night. You value things based off of what they cost you and that bronze medal cost me everything I had. To be in an impossible situation where everything is going terribly wrong and not collapse shows me what I built. Sports have a way of creating "rubber meets the road" type situations. I think that is why I like them. I say I believe things and I have values that I live by; through sport they are put on display. Not without tears, frustration and disappointment, but I kept going regardless of what was going on around me. That is what internal motivation is all about.

I waited for six minutes for the judges' decision and found myself on the Olympic podium for the third time in my career. I was thankful and proud of what I had built even if I did not get the top spot I had been gunning for.

*"Being internally motivated means that I make an intentional choice, not a reaction."*

That victory did not have a lot to do with external things. That night I relied on the lens that I had developed, on the outlook I was choosing. I was internally motivated and refused to let my circumstances dictate my decisions. It was not a need-based approach.

Being internally motivated means that I make an intentional choice, not a reaction. If you don't have a good set of principles or a plan to live from, you will constantly try to control your environment, by listening to the right warm-up song, by wearing your lucky item, trying to do enough good things that the universe rewards you, or hoping for the best. It cannot be left to chance. Strategy and hope are good things to have, but they need to be the icing on the cake, not the cake itself. The only thing you can control in life is yourself, so take some time to adjust your perspective to manage yourself well regardless of what is going on around you. If I had been looking to my circumstances to help me out that night in Russia, the story would have ended very differently, and I probably would have been found ugly crying again.

When you are building something outside yourself and contributing in a way that will outlast your ability to be relevant, it is not always glamorous. You accomplish something, but you do not get recognized for that accomplishment. It's like donating money anonymously. You are making a difference but you are the only one who knows. How your heart responds in that scenario shows you your motives. It is a good check on identity and will show you why you are doing something. If you are only looking to get recognized for your accomplishment, you are building yourself. If you enjoy seeing others succeed because of you, you are building others and something that will outlast your current influence.

## HEART TESTS

Snowboarding is an interesting sport because it is always progressing and changing, and to stay on top of your game you have to grow and progress with it. The tricks I did to win the Olympics in 2002 would not even make a final today. In 2010 I was the first women to land a 1080 in a halfpipe competition; I will give you some background on this process in a later chapter. Men had been doing it for years, but women had not progressed to that level yet. It took me years of trial and error and keeping the belief in front of me that it was physically possible for women. When I landed it in the X Games final, it was one of the top moments of my career because when I got to the bottom of the run, my peers, who were also the competition, came over and dog-piled me. It was about me, but it was also a huge moment for women in our sport. It was a step forward, worthy to be celebrated. It is easy to celebrate yourself, but that night my peers celebrated me. That image of my peers celebrating me really paints an accurate picture of competitive snowboarding. I have yet to see a sport where the relationships are protected in tension with the competitive spirit. I went on to keep that part of my run for years to come. What had once been the impossible became my normal.

I had assumed that this trick would quickly become adopted by my other competitors and become the new normal. Much to my surprise it took years before people started to implement it in their runs. In 2016, we began to see it more often and it became common in the top tier of women's competitive snowboarding.

*"Seeing other people succeed and celebrated is the ultimate heart test."*

Once people caught up to doing the trick, someone quickly took it further. In February 2016 we saw the first back-to-back 1080 in women's halfpipe competition by Chloe Kim. I had been waiting for people to catch up, and in an instant, not only did they catch up, they surpassed me. It was another huge step forward for women in snowboarding and it was the ultimate heart test for me. I had wanted to be the first woman to do back-to-back 1080s. It seemed that what I had done was not very significant anymore. I had become old news and was no longer celebrated.

Seeing other people succeed and celebrated is the ultimate heart test. How your heart responds in these types of situations will show you what motivates you. If you are no longer the main character, are you happy to be in a supporting role? The day that back-to-back 1080s were done by someone other than me, I was curious to see how my heart would react, and much to my surprise, I was more happy than jealous. I actually was not jealous at all. I celebrated, congratulated and hugged Chloe at the bottom of the pipe that day, and it was not for the cameras. As a competitive athlete, I was inspired and, therefore, will continue to pursue that trick combination. Unexpectedly, I was happy for and even proud of Chloe and where she had taken the sport.

If I had not done that first 1080, do you think she would be doing back-to-back 1080s? Did I lay the foundation for this? Did I inspire her through my accomplishments to take snowboarding further than I ever could? I think the answer to those questions is an undeniable yes! I did build something bigger than myself. I became a stepping stone for someone else to be successful. When my heart test came, I passed it. I was proud of her and proud of what I had built.

> *"To be internally motivated, we commit to a lifetime of heart tests, and sometimes we are the only ones who can understand the depth of our victories."*

I can write this out and illustrate these principles, but this cannot be boiled down to a formula. Once the why and the how of our lives become established, the lenses we are looking through are essentially developed. Things often take form in our thinking but they need to be put to a heart test to really have that "rubber meets the road" type moment. My heart passed the test that day when I was surpassed in my sport. It will not be my last heart test.

To be internally motivated, we commit to a lifetime of heart tests, and sometimes we are the only ones who can understand the depth of our victories. When we choose to be internally motivated, we also choose to take responsibility for the process; it can be vulnerable and humbling at times, but it is a joy-filled, sustainable choice to make. It is also a key to being able to embrace the journey and being okay with the process.

## REFLECTION QUESTIONS

*Who are you?*

*What are you doing?*

*Why are you doing it?*

2013 - Vail, Colorado

# CHAPTER THREE
# PREPARATION REQUIRED

*"By failing to prepare you are preparing to fail."*
*- Benjamin Franklin*

didn't qualify for my first X Games, but because I was a "good story," they let me in. My home resort in Mount Snow, Vermont, was set to host the winter X Games in 1999, and I was the local sixteen-year-old who was going to get the chance to compete on the big stage. In those days, snowboarders did not focus on one event; rather, we competed in as many as we could. I competed as a triple threat: Boardercross, Slopestyle and Halfpipe. Surprisingly, I ended up getting fourth in the Slopestyle event, which led to sponsorships and an agent wanting to sign me.

My longtime agent, Peter Carlisle, still tells this story. He and his business partner came to meet with my parents at my family's restaurant following the competition. After getting to know each other and discussing this last event, they asked me what my future plans were. Though I have no recollection of the next part of the conversation, Peter still laughs as he recalls my answer. I simply replied, "I plan on winning the Olympics." He was amused that I would be so bold to proclaim that kind of success, and was then impressed that three years later I stood atop the podium in the Salt Lake City Olympic games.

Peter has been my sports agent ever since. It makes sense now, but way back then, he took a risk. I had not accomplished much and the only reason I was a "good story" was because I was a hometown girl. The event I proclaimed I was going to win, the halfpipe, was far from a victory; I had a twelfth-place place finish in that first X Games. Based on my performance, I was not the person to bet your money on. I had no tangible or external victories and could have been overlooked. As Peter says it, once he talked to me, saw my drive and assertiveness, he knew that I was worth the risk. I had potential, and that was enough for him.

Looking back, I am a little embarrassed by that story. I think now, *Whoa, how cocky was I?* I love that I don't even remember that conversation. I have always thought of myself as rather reserved and quiet and not outspoken. I typically do more listening than talking and am an introvert by nature. So, to imagine myself boldly stating, "I plan on winning the Olympics" doesn't add up.

Where did that come from? Who was that kid? Are you sure that is what I said? I remember my teenage years being some of the most insecure times of my life, which leads me to wonder, how could I, at sixteen years old, be so sure of myself? Where did I pick that up in the midst of trying to figure out what was cool to wear or if I should put one or two straps on my backpack at school? It must have come from something more influential than my conscious choices.

Amongst all the insecurity of being a teen, one of the strongest influences a young person has in their corner is that of their upbringing. When life happens and you start to grow up, what your parents instilled in you is your default setting. We come from all different backgrounds and upbringings, and most families do their very best to set their children up to succeed. Some people have a traditional nuclear family while a great many other people grow up today with divorced parents, single mothers or fathers, or even in homes where they are not safe, invested in, or believed in. These default settings determine a lot of how teenagers react and respond to situations occurring around them. Sometimes people feel stuck in these cycles and at times perceive themselves as victims of it. While this might feel true, that line of thinking can cripple people into only believing to the level that the previous generation did about themselves, their circumstances, and the world around them.

---

*"My parents' belief that I could shoot for the moon and actually make it was my reality."*

---

The most noticeable value my parents instilled in me was that of hard work. I watched them work hard at everything they did and often make sacrifices that I didn't understand. I am so grateful to have witnessed such good work ethic, and it shaped me in so many ways. Through hard work, my mother and father instilled in me the reality that I could do anything. They were not unique in a sense that they told me I could be or do anything I wanted to; perhaps the unique part was that I actually believed them. I think most parents tell their little girl that she can do anything she puts her mind to.

I believe the confidence I had, that bold statement I made about my future, came from that place of an internal structure I wasn't even aware of. My parents' belief that I could shoot for the moon and actually make it there was my reality; I didn't know any better than to believe them. I attribute a great deal of my internal fortitude to them because I never thought there was anything I couldn't do.

The irony of it all came when I told my parents what I planned to do with my life. When the words "I want to be a professional snowboarder" came out of my mouth, their response was simple: "Oh Kelly, anything but that." As quickly as they said it, I recounted to them their promise to me because it was my default setting. Their apprehension may seem silly, but you have to remember, it was the year 1998, before snowboarding was cool and definitely before it was a career goal. It was not even a popular Olympic sport yet, and it was far from mainstream. If that wasn't bad enough, it is a sport, that by its nature, has physical risks and to be the best requires risks and literally beating out the competition to obtain that top spot. In short, it was not a sustainable career for a sensible daughter to pursue.

After many discussions, tears, and some compromise, we settled on a one-year trial period. I had one year to make it happen. I could defer college for one year to prove to them that this was a sustainable career, that I could be the best, and that I could make a future out of snowboarding. We were not believing in what I had done in the past; Peter, my parents and I were going all in on the potential we knew was inside and hoped I could access. My parents first gave me that one year because they believed in me. I got to explore my potential because they saw something in me, something that could be there, something that I would find if given the opportunity.

## HOW DO YOU SEE POTENTIAL?

The lens you see your potential through is molded by your own perceptions as well as the perceptions of those around you. Potential can be defined many ways, but I like to think of it as a mix of talent, ability, and belief.

Surround yourself with people who believe in you and who believe in who you want to become. I always say that behind every great athlete is a team of great people. I am a product of people investing and believing in me. The lens that I see myself and my potential through is made clearer when I surround myself with people who believe in me. That belief only strengthens my talent and ability.

Now, it can go both ways. If you have people around you who do not champion you, your potential or talents, you may want to reevaluate who your "family" is. The people that we surround ourselves with have the ability to influence us. There is the positive example of my parents believing in me, but imagine if they told me I was worthless. My default setting would have told me I was worthless as opposed to the one that said "nothing is impossible." The people around us have the ability to influence us, and they can shape our beliefs and in turn our actions.

I have a friend who has one of the craziest laughs I have ever heard. If I have not hung out with her in a while and we start laughing, I am always taken aback by her head-back, eyes-closed, mouth-open cackle. People are always like, "What is that noise and where is it coming from?" After spending only a little bit of time with her, I hear that loud cackle and I am like, "What is that, and where is it coming from?" Much to my surprise it is me. In just a short amount of time together, I somehow pick up her laugh. If we can pick up behaviors and little things from the people by just spending a few days with them, imagine what we can pick up from people when we do life with them?

*"If we do not believe we can be great, we will not have the courage to actually be great."*

Our actions are an extension of our beliefs. If we do not believe we can be great, we will not have the courage to actually be great. In addition to surrounding ourselves with the right people, we need to also be willing to take feedback, criticism and even setbacks to propel us forward. Everyone celebrates the highlights of their life and social media will be the first to tell us this. We all know that everyone's life is not that glamorous all the time, but it seems like it. It is not what happens to us that directs our life; rather, it is what we do with what happens to us that directs it.

It's sometimes those moments what we get shut down, fall down or flat out fail that shape us the most. I have never been the best snowboarder;

people have been better than me my entire life. I have been with Burton snowboards for the last seventeen years. They have invested more in me than any other company and I am eternally grateful that I get to represent them. Before I was a Burton Girl, I was another nameless, faceless, ambitious snowboarder with a rejection letter from them. One year before I finally received sponsorship, I sent my biography with hopes of getting noticed. Back then, we did not have a YouTube link to send them putting on display our best moments; we had a printed word document and some average photos taken by our moms to submit. My best friend had just gotten picked up by Burton and I thought, *Well I am almost that good. I should submit my bio too.* While she was getting the freshest boards from them, I got a rejection letter stating that I was not at a high enough level for their support.

---

*"I think I was paralyzed by
the pressure of being on top."*

---

I could have taken it and let it shape me negatively. I could have given it a big voice in my life leading to an enrollment in my local community college. Instead, I listened to my family, the ones who believed in me. I chose to work harder and continued to believe in my potential. I knew it would only be a matter of time until they saw what I knew.

## POTENTIAL DOES NOT EQUAL SUCCESS

Many people think potential will automatically lead to success. Unfortunately, it is not that simple. I found out the hard way that is not how that works after the Salt Lake Games. I was in unfamiliar territory on the other side of an Olympic gold, wondering what "next" would look like. I had actually accomplished what I set out to do, so I did not know what the future looked like for me. The uncertainty of my heart and the expectations of others were fighting for position in my life and it was rather overwhelming. After years of having a clear vision, I actually found myself visionless. My default kicked in and I decided to just work or go through the motions. Going through the motions meant I did only what was expected of me and nothing more. At the time, I was unaware why I had this reaction to success, but looking back now, I think I was paralyzed by the pressure of being on top. I did not know what I wanted to do and had no idea what to do after accomplishing my goal. I should have had vision for myself; instead I was overwhelmed with what people wanted me to do.

*"The pressure of the top didn't propel me forward; it actually helped me settle for average."*

Heading into the 2006 Olympic qualifiers, I was still in no-man's land in my mind and in my sport. The Olympic hype is always about the returning gold medalist, including dramatic language like, "Defending Olympic Champion," and the "greatest of all time." For the first time in my life, I was aware that my internal drive was nowhere to be found. It caught me off guard. It wasn't that I did not want to snowboard or go to the Olympics again, but I did not know how to deal with the pressure I was now experiencing. That pressure had built over the four years since Salt Lake and was coming to a head at the qualifying events prior to the Games. I found myself performing poorly at the qualifying events, which is expected for someone who is going through the motions.

The pressure of the top didn't propel me forward; it actually helped me settle for average. I was racking up many 3rd and 4th place finishes keeping me right in the contention for a spot on the Olympic team. I didn't even realize that I was at risk for not making the team until the final qualifier. It came down to me in a "have to" situation; I "had to" land to make the team. Not only did I need to land, I needed a 2nd place finish or better to slide into that 4th spot on the U.S. Olympic team. Knowing all of this, I fell on my first run. I had one more shot to make it and I just squeaked in there by the skin of my teeth. The threat of not making the Olympic team made me kick it into gear. Sometimes the threat of not having something is a good way to determine what you do want. I decided I wanted to be an Olympian again; I wanted to win.

> *"Playing it safe is always a risk;*
> *it comes with the risk of regret."*

I went to Torino, Italy, a few weeks later and began training at the 2006 Olympic Games. The more I rode, the better I got. I somehow decided to wake up from my slumber and counted myself in; after all, I was the defending champ and I was determined to rise to the occasion. On the second day of the Olympics, I breezed through qualifiers and found myself in the top spot heading into finals. I knew that if I landed the run I wanted to, I would fit the bill and be that champion everyone wanted me to be; it would only take thirty seconds. The problem was that I was not in a position to risk it all, I was not consistent, and I was far from polished. After all, I barely made the team. I knew I had the potential to win, but it was going to be too risky to lay it on the line both runs. I thought I could do a safe run that was consistent and lock up a podium spot, then go for the kill shot with run two.

Playing it safe is always a risk; it comes with the risk of regret, which is one of the most unsettling scenarios you can manufacture in your life. I was simply not up to speed. I did not have the consistency needed as I had not decided that I was there to win until the week of the Games. With run one done, I was sitting in third place. I decided then and there that was good enough for me to go for it on my final run. I knew I had to decide what I was going to be happy with at the end of the day.

I knew I had the potential to win. I was strapped in ready to go for my final run, and my coach looked at me and held up four fingers. I knew exactly what it meant: I was no longer in 3rd place. I was no longer in a position to medal based on my prior "safe" run.

At this point, I was dead set on going for it, and that is just what I did. It was all or nothing and I was confident in my decision. I did the best run anyone had seen in women's halfpipe snowboarding history—that is until my last trick. In order to get maximum points for a run, under no circumstances can you "sit down." Well, that is exactly what I did when I landed my final trick off balance and skidded across the finish line on my backside. I watched my podium hopes disappear for another four years, Americans would not sweep the podium, and I would disappear into the background for a season of life as the girl who couldn't get it done when it counted and remained in 4th place.

The Torino Games is a difficult story to recount because it was one of the most devastating events of my life. I was given thirty seconds to go for it and I lost it in the last two. It did not work out for me. I had to wait four more years for a chance to redeem myself. There were too many tears to count over the next few seasons of life. I did not regret my decision making that day; I made the right decision but I did regret that I did not prepare before the actual event. I learned a very important lesson that day. I learned that there is a very big difference between having potential and being prepared.

Even though Torino was one of the most heart-wrenching moments of my career, I knew it was also perhaps the most significant moment. This defeat caused me to realize what I actually wanted. It made me look inside and see what Kelly wanted beyond other people's expectations and beyond my own fear of failure. Through not achieving what I had hoped, I finally knew what I wanted. I realized that *I never wanted to be at the edge of my ability level ever again*. I did not want to have to have the run of my life to win. I wanted to prepare in such a way that my potential could be met and exceeded at any given time because I was ready to do my best always. For the first time in years I knew what I wanted, and I would spend the next four years investing in my potential so I would not have my back up against the ropes again.

## PREPARATION

One of the biggest realizations that came out of that defeat was the identification that sometimes even I wanted *instant gratification*. Instant gratification, at times, defines aspects of our culture as people living in the 21st century. When we look around, there are not too many things that require us to wait. If we don't want to cook, we simply go to a restaurant. If we don't want to sit and eat, we can find a drive-thru. If we cannot be bothered to leave our house, we can always order in. This cycle of needs being met instantly continually communicates to us that everything should be done by now.

> *"We have removed all the wait time from our lives in the name of efficiency and convenience."*

From the way we get our media to the fact that you can order things online and they can be delivered the same day, we want it *now*. In culture, we see it take many shapes beyond shopping and finding a good place to eat. It exists with diets, where people are told they can lose weight fast without having to work hard. We have removed all wait time from our lives in the name of efficiency and convenience. How convenient is it really? What does it communicate to us? Just because our culture has changed does not mean that the conventional way that you gain things should change.

Sadly, this cultural shift has led to a society that has unrealistic expectations about many things that require process. What happens to

*"Good preparation prevents regrets."*

things that take time? They become valuable. As people age, they often say, "I'm like a good bottle of wine; I just get better with age." A good bottle of wine often becomes more expensive with age too. Why is that? Because you can't get it any other way; it takes time and time is expensive but necessary to get the best. The older the vintage, the more money it will cost, and cost correlates directly with value. The more expensive things are the more value they hold. Some of the most valuable things you will get in life will not come instantly; they will come through a process that usually takes time. If we short ourselves in our preparation, we will feel like we are cramming for a test. We may remember the first few answers, but in the end, we will fail. In 2006, I crammed for the test, I had the potential, but I did not do the preparation and I failed.

Good preparation prevents regrets. If you prepare there will be no, "I wish I had..." or "If only..." It holds you accountable to your dream and responsible for the outcome. You get to determine the success of the dream. Preparation is a key to impacting the world around you instead of having it impact you. People ask me often, "How far out from the Olympics do you start getting ready?" Now that I realize what is required, I say, "The moment I am done with the last Games." If I am given four years to prepare, I want to use all the time I have and use it wisely.

## DESTINATION DISEASE

I spent four years getting ready for the 2010 Vancouver Olympics with one of my good friends, four years preparing for that moment. Both of us made sacrifices, worked harder, and spent more time than most people to get ready. We were on the U.S. Olympic Halfpipe Team; we were the best in the world and had a lot riding on our shoulders. We knew this was supposed to be one of the greatest moments of our lives. Like most great moments, they are over before we know what happened.

> *"We are made for process, going on journeys of discovery and progress; it is up to us to be faithful in the waiting."*

After our big event, we were in the finish area, and my friend looked at me and asked me this question, "Are you so glad it is over?" I looked at her a little confused as I thought it was a strange question. It wasn't that I didn't know what she was talking about; the Olympics are not for the faint of heart. I was hit with the reality that we work a lifetime for this moment, it is the very moment where we get to live out our dream, and there was someone glad when it would all be done. What showed in her relief reflected to me my own experience just four years before when I just wanted to run away from Torino and away from the pressure. In that moment, I learned something about myself: I realized I was finally competing for the right reasons. I finally passed the heart test that sports so often bring to the surface.

My motivation was exposed in that conversation. I was not glad it was over, nor was I relieved. I felt privileged to have been part of an event that 1 in every 5,000,000 Americans will ever get to experience. I was thankful. I realized that my destination, the Olympics, was no longer driving me. I was in such a different spot than most of my teammates, both in my career and in my life. Most Olympians decide not to finish the competition season in an Olympic year because the Olympics are the focus of their career that year. After Vancouver, I actually went to my coaches and asked them if it was alright for me to finish out the season. I was happy to continue on because for the first time in my life, I was not treating the Olympics as a destination. I was not glad it was over; I was just glad I got to be part.

Destination disease is not a problem exclusive to athletes. If you are breathing, then there is a good chance that you are looking forward to something happening in your life. Maybe you are waiting to find the love of your life or the perfect job. For some people, they think about the day when their ship comes in, all the stars align, and all their dreams come true. Unfortunately, until this happens, they will never be happy. It is possible that someone is letting life pass them by waiting to get somewhere they envision before they can be happy and never enjoy the journey along the way. It is impossible to sustain a lifestyle driven solely by arrival at a destination; it will always disappoint. We were not created to arrive one day and everything magically becomes perfect. We were made for process, going on journeys of discovery and progress; it is up to us to be faithful in the waiting.

## REFLECTION QUESTIONS

*Where do you see potential in your life?*

*What steps can you take to intentionally grow into that potential?*

*What happens when you are caught up in the destination and miss the journey?*

2013 – Mount Hood, Oregon

# CHAPTER FOUR
# RAISING THE BAR

*"Only those who risk going too far can possibly find out how far one can go."*

*T. S. Elliot*

n competitive snowboarding, it is all about the next best thing. If you have ever seen an X Games you know there is always someone trying to break a new record, and every year, records are being broken. I knew if I wanted to break boundaries and be the best, I needed to establish a really high normal, a normal that pushed the edges of the sport and my own limitations. I couldn't just allow myself to be basic; I had to set a goal to achieve something outside the box. In the process, my basic run had to be perfect and excellent. It had to somehow be better than my competitors' most difficult runs so that when my easy run was done, I was already at the top. Essentially, to free myself up to go after reaching an impossible goal, I had to raise my own bar. Not because of what other people were doing, but because of what I wanted to do. If I was going to do my job well, win the event, and achieve what was in my heart, I had to make everything better. Accomplishing a goal is about more than landing one trick; it is about everything being top notch, freeing myself up to take big risks.

Until 2011, no woman even attempted a 1080 in a halfpipe competition even though men had been doing them for more than ten years. I knew it was possible, and because it was the next logical progression for me, I wanted to learn it. A 1080 is three full rotations in the halfpipe, it is 180 degrees more than any woman had done successfully in an event. The trick just before you reach a 1080 is a 900, also called a 9. I had been doing front 9s for years and spinning that direction was my greatest strength, so I knew I had something to build on.

I have never struggled with the concept of equality- I have always believed women can do the same things men can do. How we get there is where the differences lie. In my experience, if you tell a guy to try something he will go and do it, maybe not successfully, but do it nonetheless. Women, on the other hand, tend to be a bit more calculated, more likely to attempt something once we understand it. If I understand how to do a trick, only then will I go send it.

I tried my first 1080 in 2005; I landed my first 1080 in 2011. It was not an easy task. Yes, it took six years to complete. When I started learning, I would only do them when I was having a good day, when everything was working. I would get up the courage and just send it, hoping for the best. I think that is why it took me six years to finally land one. It was not a question of how to do it; I knew that. But I only attempted them based on my feelings that day. Six years in snowboarding equates to about 800 days of actual time on snow. As I only attempted a 1080 when I felt like it, I lost so much time. Doing things only when we feel like it becomes a problem in many areas of life, mainly when we are trying to reach a goal or attempting something new.

After a few years of that approach and having no success, I thought I should try something different. After all, the definition of insanity is trying the same thing over and over again and expecting different results. I was most definitely not getting a different result, and landing on my side a million times was becoming too painful to continue.

One day I decided, today is the day. It was a simple adjustment, but I

*"You can't wait for the stars to align*
*and expect to just have it all work out."*

made a simple decision I would do a 1080 that day when I went out on the hill. I kept it in mind all day and worked toward it in small ways. It sounds so basic looking back on it; my coach and I still laugh about the way I found resolve. It is a simple principle: if you want to be able to do something, you intentionally have to set out to do it. You can't wait for the stars to align and expect to just have it all work out. To be honest, many approach competitive snowboarding in a way that says, "I only do it when I have to," which means, "I only do my most difficult tricks when it is an X Games final, not because I want to but because I have to." Many live their everyday lives like this too. I was familiar with this mindset but tired of the approach. I wanted to be intentional.

Achieving a goal starts with a process of evaluation. Once I targeted what I wanted to do, I could then approach how to do it. The question became, "How am I going to progress and achieve my goal of landing a 1080 and win the event at the same time?" I had to be strategic. I had to make sure my basics were covered, and at the same time, not count on my run to be my great accomplishment.

At the X Games in 2011, I landed my first 1080; it was one of the highlights of my career. Even though it was almost seven years ago, I remember it like it was yesterday. I knew it would be a great risk for the outcome of my competition, but it seemed worth it even though I had yet to land a 1080 in an event, or at all. It's one thing to learn something, and then another thing to do it consistently so you can insert it into your competition run. In snowboarding events, specifically the halfpipe, we get multiple runs. At the end of the day, only one of those runs will count. My plan that day was to land a good enough run for the win and then use my throwaway runs to land the 1080. Simple enough, except I actually had to land the 1080—minor detail. Seemed like a good plan: I could not only win the X Games but do a trick that no woman has ever done before—yeah, great plan, Kelly.

My coach and I took a good look at my runs, looked at where I was in my season, and we thought I was in a good place to go after this goal. I would go out in practice and build up to my contest run, and if I could land that perfectly three times in a row, then I could move on. Getting to practice my 1080 was like a little reward for landing my contest run consistently in practice; not surprisingly, my contest runs took me longer than expected to land perfectly. My practice days slipped by without me even attempting one 1080.

On the last day of practice, most of my competitors had already gone home. They were done for the day, and they were going to rest up for the main event. I had a different goal in mind. It was not just about winning that event for me; it was about taking my snowboarding forward. I was more interested in landing a new trick than having the perfect polished run or even standing atop a podium. The balance between perfection and progression is a delicate one, and I was walking a tightrope that year. All the struggles aside, I was finally ready to risk perfection for the sake of progression.

I knew I had one or maybe two runs left before the starters would close practice and send everyone home. At that moment, I landed my perfect contest run for the third time and knew that it was now or never. I went to the snowmobile as fast as I could to get back to the top. I went over to my coach and he knew exactly what I was thinking. He said, "If you want to do it before the event, you have to do it now."

It was going to be my last trick in my run, so an early fall would spoil the opportunity. I would need to hold it together all the way to my last hit. I find when I have something really difficult to do, my mind only thinks about that one thing. In snowboarding, much like life, you can never lose your focus; you can easily focus on the wrong thing at the wrong time. I needed to not forget how to do the basic things on my way to my big goal, I needed to be on my feet with enough speed and composure to attempt something that had never been done before.

As I made my way to the bottom of the run my mind raced ahead; I tried to reel it in and stay focused on the task at hand. I was at the last hit and much like the many times I had tried it before, I came up short and landed square on my butt. It was not the reward I was looking for, but it gave me an idea. For the first time, it was not going to be something that I just throw in at the end of the run. What if I tried it up higher in the run? What if I tried it second hit? I would not be trying to fit it in, and I could carry it down the wall, thus putting my weight forward and perhaps forward enough to finish the rotation on my feet. After all, I was doing it intentionally, so why couldn't I do it up high in my run, like I meant it?

Time was ticking down. I raced to the snowmobile and practically ran up the stairs to get back to the top in time. I pleaded with the starter and asked for one more run. They held it open for me, and I think the rush of everything almost helped me not overthink it. I told my coach my plan: I would try it second hit. I would take some line down the wall and expect to land. One, two, three...it came around, and much to my surprise I landed on my feet. I was so surprised I landed it that I almost fell into the other wall and then went to the bottom of the pipe. My friends were there in disbelief, as was I. I had done what no woman had ever done before.

> *"It was the perfect meeting of courage and preparation."*

Snowboarding is a funny thing because if you do a trick wrong, there are big consequences and things end in a big crash. On the other hand, if everything goes to plan, and you land that trick, it is almost anti-climactic as you ride away surprised by the lack of eventfulness. I rode away surprised to be on my feet. I was surprised along with everyone else that day. I had done my contest runs perfectly and progressed all at the same time; it was the perfect meeting of courage and preparation. Now all I had to do was land it in an actual competition.

My plan was going perfectly. The X Games world of "firsts" was a buzz to see if I would be the first woman to land a 1080 live on network television. A clip from practice was on the Internet, and it kept getting played on ESPN in anticipation of it happening at the main event. Even so, I decided I would stick to the plan—land my first run, the whole point in raising my own bar. The 1080 was a secondary goal. I wanted to be able to use the event setting to progress only after I had done what I needed to do to win the event. My safe stock run had to be better than everyone's best, or at least it had to be my best. After that, the only way to push myself would be to go for the 1080.

*"I tend to simplify things in big moments."*

As we pulled into the parking lot at the base of Aspen mountain, we could see the halfpipe illuminated for the X Games final. It was surreal, but all I could come up with to say was, "I'm into it." My team manager at the time looked at me and laughed, "That's it? You are into it?" I tend to simplify things in big moments. The big moments in life are not made for details and effort—that time is better spent executing the plan. I knew what I wanted to do, and I had done the work ahead of time to make this dream happen, or at least given myself the best shot at making it happen. I planned to win the event and then make history. It can seem arrogant to say that; I think there is a difference between arrogance and confidence. It is a precarious line to walk, but you need confidence to be at your best, and I planned on being my best that night. This was not some kind of feeling I had that evening; it was an achievement almost seven years in the making.

There is an approach to our competition that says, "Do the easy run first and the hard run second." In halfpipe, you get to throw away one or even two of your runs. It is considered wise to do the run you feel comfortable with and get a good score first, then go for broke on the second and third runs. If you don't land your easy run, you limit yourself. If that happens, you are then stuck with the dilemma of doing your safe run to get a podium position or doing your progressive run to see what you are capable of accomplishing. I was not going to change this approach, just tweak it a little. The basic run would become the winning run whether I landed it first or second run; and if everything went to plan, I would get to push myself without sacrificing my position or results.

My first run was landed perfectly. I find that having a contest run more difficult can make the most difficult tricks I can do seem easier. I got the score I wanted, and I hoped it would hold up for the win. I was resolved that no matter what the other competitors did that night, I was going to stick to my plan. Because of the effort required and the setting of the run, I was still planning on doing the 1080 on my last hit. Even though that had not proved successful in practice, it still was the most logical approach to take when putting a new trick in my run. I went up for that last hit and like many times before I found myself on my side in the flat bottom. I instantly knew what I needed to do: I had to move it higher up in the run. The middle of the run was no place for a new trick, but that is how I was able to do it in practice, and I needed to do it like that now. I went to the top and my coach looked at me and said, "You have to do it second hit. That is the only way it is going to work." We were on the same page, and it was time for my last run of the night.

I knew dropping in that I had already won the event. My plan was working, only one more part needed to fall into place: making history. Apart from my coach, Ricky, no one knew I was going to do the 1080 higher up in my run. So, when I went up, did the trick, and landed on my feet, everyone was amazed. They had been waiting for it on my last hit. I remember watching it on TV later that night and the announcers were silent; it took them until a few tricks later in my run to express their excitement for what I had accomplished.

It was a historic night for me and for women's snowboarding. It is one thing to celebrate yourself, but when I got down to the bottom of the run my competitors tackled me. It wasn't just about me; it was about the sport and we all celebrated that. I went on to land my 1080 five times in competition that year, never once needing it to win the event. I did my stock run that would place me in first and then went on to push myself with a 1080, slowly making it my new normal. My goal that year and every year since has been to raise my own bar. In doing that, I set myself up to find the place where preparation and progression meet.

I happened to life that night; life didn't happen to me. I was intentional in my pursuit, and my pursuit paid off. No circumstance or limitation dictated the decisions I made, and our sport progressed because I was prepared and courageous. It could have been anyone, but I am glad it was me.

## CALCULATED RISKS

It may have looked like I was risking life and limb to learn that new trick. We snowboarders are not always the risk-takers we are labeled as in the mainstream media. I think the term that better suits us is "calculated risk-takers." I was risking life and limb quite literally, but it was the next step in progression for me with my snowboarding. There was really no other option if I wanted to keep going. In taking the risk, there was a lot more than people realize on the line: my income, sponsorships, future, or more dramatically my ability to have a functional life. It was a risk I was willing to take, and each one of us has to ask ourselves many times throughout our lives, is it worth it?

So, what does it look like for you to calculate your risk? What foundation do you have to set in place in your life to strategically go after your dreams? What does it look like to progress in life? In business? It isn't different for you than it was for me. It looks like raising your own bar.

As with my choice to land a new trick, you also have to raise your own normal and be intentional to go after your dreams. The same principles will produce results in your own life.

## MOTIVATION TO TAKE RISKS

Competition usually causes us to raise our standards. This can definitely be good. Some athletes say it's the competition days that push them the most, or they decided that because everyone else was doing so great it gave them permission to be great too. This is helpful if you need motivation, if you want to do things that other people are doing. The competition-driven mindset leads people to be part of the pack, not the leader of the pack, or even the best version of oneself.

The bottom line is that you have to be your own motivator. If you want to do something no one has done before you, the best motivator of you is you! You have to become your biggest inspiration. I realized that I could not look to my competitors or my circumstances to decide what tricks to do or what I could accomplish. I could not wait for competition days to bring out my hard tricks, wait for permission to try something big. It started with me. I had to raise my own bar and make my hard runs become easier and easier so that I had room to learn new things.

Why would I need to make something that is difficult easy? If I could make something that was hard for me my new standard, I would not sacrifice my income or my position in the events at the expense of my progression. So, the "risky" part of the equation starts to disappear.

I knew that the more I did my hard runs, the easier they would become. Every day on the hill, I set out to do my hardest contest run. No one was pushing me to do that; in fact, a move like that is rare in the sports world. I remember being at a halfpipe camp in Colorado just before the X Games. We only had the pipe privately early in the morning, and I was determined to do my contest run every day. I was doing 900s and back to back 720s in the dark and icy early morning hours. My teammates

---

*"If you don't know where you want to go, someone else will decide that for you."*

---

would make comments like, "Wow, someone means business today." Even, "Kelly, you are really going for it today." I had a plan. I knew what my normal needed to be and it was not dependent upon what other people were doing. Every day I would try my X Games finals run. By becoming familiar with it, the run was no longer special or unique and the difficulty of it decreased. I knew in order to make my risk less risky one I needed to raise my own bar. It was in the practice times that I could take the risk. I could prepare and be ready when I needed to be.

We explored in an earlier chapter what it looks like to let your circumstances determine the choices you make, and it needs to be considered in this context. At the end of the day, if you don't know where you want to go, someone else will decide that for you. This is where the line between leaders and followers is established. By setting the bar high, you get to steer the ship and not have the ship steered for you.

Here are some things to remember as you begin taking calculated risks. Each of these categories is something I remember in my life daily as I pursue progress.

## OTHER PEOPLE DON'T DEFINE MY DESTINY

I set the bar and I don't look to other people to define my decisions. Although it is important to have people in your corner, be coachable, and get input, you must decide for yourself what you are willing to commit to doing and not compromise. The people in your corner do not get to decide where you are going. You never want someone to have a bigger piece of the decision-making pie in your life than you do. I never want my vision to get diluted or even polluted. I need to know where I want to go, then let people rally around me to see my vision through to the end. Only you can define what success is and what it looks like for you to get there.

> *"What we are building should determine what we are doing."*

I have done a lot of things that were considered unconventional in the snowboarding world. Thankfully, I am in a culture where we embrace individualism and authenticity. Even still, at times as I approached goals differently, I was criticized for my actions. Outside observers, however, didn't know what I was building. My teammates could have perceived my daily finals runs as a chest-puffing arrogant move, but for me I was raising my own standard, not trying to prove how good I was. What we are building should determine what we are doing.

As every year ticks by, I seem to be the oldest I have ever been; I know, observant. Snowboarding is traditionally a young person's sport. I am in fact two times the age of many of my competitors. Therefore, it is natural that I approach things differently, and with the brief lifespan of the sport of snowboarding, many people in the industry still cringe when you call it a sport at all. It is more fondly looked upon as a lifestyle; that outlook is embedded very deeply in our culture.

Everyone is going to have an opinion, but it is up to you to take all those things and decipher what is going to be the best combination of options for you to be successful. Only you and the people closest to you know what you are building, and you have to define the best way to get there.

## RESPOND - DON'T REACT

It would have been easy for me to be offended many times on my journey. Let's be real, we have many opportunities to be offended in life, period. It is our responsibility to take feedback, take what is good, and kick the rest to the curb. Even the most well-intentioned people can give the worst advice. You are the only one who is responsible for your dream and making it happen. Be aware of what you let into your thoughts, your mind, your heart, and even your body. You can choose to be responsive and not reactionary. Know what you are going to do ahead of time and how you will face challenges along the way. By doing this, you don't have to come up with a plan or decision on the spot and are less likely to be swayed by people's opinions and challenging circumstances.

> *"You are the only one who is responsible*
> *for your dream and making it happen."*

Think of it as one of those important talks many parents give to their kids. "Sweetheart, if someone offers you an alcoholic beverage, what are you going to do?" It seems funny and awkward coming from your mom, but you are eternally thankful that she forced you to come up with a plan the moment you were put on the spot. The choices you make and the things you do on your journey won't always be valued by everyone. You know what is going to be of value to you and your dream, so stick to it regardless of what other people say who don't have a place of influence in your life.

## BE INTENTIONAL

Intentional growth happens because I have a goal. I do things to grow because I want to, not because I have to. Being intentional puts the ball in your court. When you are intentional, you become less susceptible to people's opinions, to the latest trend, or to everyone else's normal. It allows you to grow and even outgrow your friends, coworkers or competitors.

New Zealand is one of my favorite places to travel to. As it is their winter during our North American summer, we end up traveling there most every year to chase the snow. We stay in the most spectacular little town in the middle of the South Island called Wanaka. They have one of the world's most famous and most photographed trees. If you search "Wanaka tree" you will see why. It's a small, normal looking tree, but the unique feature that makes it so famous is how it literally grows straight out of the lake. It's away from the shore, and there are no other trees around it. Even when you look at the shore and all the trees there, they don't compare to the little tree that has planted itself out in the middle of the lake.

I always try to imagine how it got there. Were there other trees around it at one point? Was the lake level lower and this tree was so rooted that it somehow survived? Could it possibly have sprouted up from the water? I may never know how it got there but it is plain to see that it has no plans to go anywhere else. It doesn't care that there are no other trees that look like it and no other trees growing there. Even when the water rose around it, it stayed steadfast in its growth. This tree is such a good example for us. That's how we should be in our pursuit of growth. In order to grow we have to first want to grow, and sometimes we should learn to stand firm when the water rises around us. It may not be normal, but sometimes standing out is a good thing.

## REFLECTION QUESTIONS

*On a scale of 1–10, how much do you challenge yourself in life?*

*What risks are you taking toward a dream?*

*What happens if you refuse to take a risk?*

*How do you "raise your own bar" or motivate yourself?*

*2007 - Snowpark, New Zealand*

# CHAPTER FIVE
# TRANSITION

*"Often when you think you're at the end of one thing, you're at the beginning of something else."*
*–Mr. Rodgers*

Success looks different in different seasons. If we never actually arrive in life, we find ourselves constantly in a specific season or in a type of transition to the next one. Things can and always do change, so our definition of success requires flexibility. What was successful for you in one season may not work in the next one. As our seasons change, so does our definition of success. As I survey my life, I find dozens, if not hundreds, of examples of how seasons change and how success looks different with each change. Situations and circumstances will always vary, but transitions cause us to redefine everything. We transition in and out of it from time to time with different ways and means of measurement.

Over the course of my career, I have had very few injuries. Traditionally, we think of snowboarding as a high impact sport where you are constantly battling injuries. We imagine injuries to be the fruit from this "extreme" sport. People always ask me questions like, "You must be

---

*"As our seasons change, so does our definition of success."*

---

hurt all the time" or, "How many bones have you broken?" The all too common question in interviews is, "What has been your worst injury?" Until 2016, I really did not have much of an answer.

Over my 17-year professional career I wound up with several injuries—most of them minor. I had a few concussions in the early years before I learned how to fall properly. That is an art that I finally mastered. As far as surgeries go, I had a right knee scope and a left wrist scope. These scopes, or arthroscopic procedures, cleaned up some torn ligaments—very minor in the big scheme of things. The best way to gauge it is that I never actually had to pull out of an event due to injury, though I won't say it's been all rainbows and unicorns. I have spent enough time in the gym, on the spin bike, taking recovery ice baths and on the physical therapy table each week to equate to a part-time job. I never really had an injury that required any extended time off snow to recover—until the 2015-2016 competition season.

In the summer of 2015, I started to get lower back pain. Nothing major, but it was the first time I ever really experienced random pain. As a 32-year-old professional snowboarder I was wondering if, at some point, I would start to feel these random aches and pains I heard so much about. Though the pain was uncomfortable, I did not think much of it and kept up with my workouts. After a few weeks, I started to get nerve pain in my glute, which started to get irritated during my standard workouts. I let my medical staff know what was going on, then went to the U.S. Snowboard team headquarters in Utah to get an MRI. Upon arriving there and being evaluated, we decided I had a technique issue with some of my workouts that was contributing to this pain. We adjusted my program, I treated it with P.T. and rest, and I went on my way.

Unfortunately, once I was home I did not find much relief from my pain. It was now October and my season was fast approaching. Normally, heading into my season, I am coming off my most intense training weeks and start my first event strong and confident. Because of the injury, I was not training at all; I was spending time resting. I did not know if I was even going to be able to ride down to the pipe, let alone have that strength and confidence I was so used to when I competed. My coaches and I did not know what to do, so I opted to go to Colorado and get on snow and go from there. There was no way to know how my body would feel until I got out there and got in the pipe.

Much to everyone's surprise, we were able to manage the pain and I was able to ride. I made it through the first two events mildly hopeful. I thought, *Well, after the Christmas break perhaps I will be able to gain some of the strength I was lacking from missing my preseason prep.* In mid-January at the next event, all of the competitors battled the weather, causing us to have limited practice. I have a tendency to overdo it at times, so this was good for me as I was not feeling 100 percent yet. On finals day, I played to my strengths and went for it with no practice. My experience paid off for me that day, and I walked away with the win. I thought to myself, *This is more like it! Maybe I will be able to make this season happen after all.*

That thinking was put to rest as I approached the upcoming X Games. Going in, I felt like I had it together enough to at least fake my way through this season. The event was not going to be easy, but I was making the most of the days leading up to it. The second practice day I got a call from my dad. It was one of those calls that you get and you immediately know by the introduction that something is terribly wrong. My grandmother had been battling dementia and a few other medical conditions for almost ten years. She finally lost that battle and died that day at 87 years old. My family had all said our goodbyes and knew this was going to be in the near future, but loss is loss, and my heart was grieving the loss of my last living grandparent.

I stood there the next day at practice feeling hollow and worn out, tired from crying and sore from the back-to-back weeks of events on my hurting, unprepared body. I did not know what else to do but to compete. The only thing I could do was to "Just. Keep. Going." I told my coaches that I was not going to pull out of the event; I was going to ride. From there, I was clueless of how to handle the situation. I opted not to let the media in on my loss as I thought it would only add external pressure, expectation, and attention I did not want.

As we entered the women's final in Aspen, the snow was just starting to come down. By the time we had our first runs, it was snowing so hard we could not see the bottom of the pipe at times. As with every crummy situation, I said to myself, "If I have a personal life crisis and the event is going to happen in a blizzard, this is a great opportunity." I said it and I hoped it but was too depleted that day to make it happen. I was not able to put a run together that was worth anything, and I failed to place top 3 in an event for the first time in four years. It was the first time in ten years that I failed to make the podium at X Games. I was crushed emotionally, mentally and physically that day. I lost, and I lost badly.

The pain didn't end there, however; I made it through one more event in Utah, snuck on the podium for personal redemption and went to Norway for the next X Games stop. On the second night of practice, I was working on getting my 10s together. I had come up short on some, and things were not working the way I was hoping—seemed to be the theme for my season so far. I thought I would try to get one under my belt so I could go into the final with some confidence and momentum. I got forward a little bit as I hit the wall and it caused me to go straighter than I had hoped. But since I was wound up for the trick, I knew the only thing to do was to go with it, hope for the best, and take the fall. I thought I would just be sore but okay; after all, I aborted that trick more than a hundred times before. Unfortunately, this time the tip of my board got stuck underneath me at a weird angle and, instead of my body bending and absorbing the impact, I felt something pull in my pelvis— in my bone. It burned and tears filled my eyes under my goggles. As

I lay there in the pipe, my mind was flooded with all the possibilities. Had it finally happened? Is this a serious injury? I gripped my hamstring knowing something was very wrong.

I knew anyone who saw me lying in the flat-bottom of the pipe would be worried, so I did my best to get it together. I stood up and rode down to the bottom of the pipe under my own power. I was hurt. I did not know how bad, but I knew this time, I was definitely hurt. I went over to the U.S. team doctor and he checked me out. Nothing could be done on the spot, so I headed for the bus back to the hotel. I sat on the bus with so many more thoughts: *What if I am too old? What if my body is breaking down? Why is nothing going well?* I know my body and I knew that this time it was not just a bruise or a strain.

For the first time in my career, it crossed my mind that I might be at the end. I cried myself to sleep that night wondering if I had just flown to Norway for the scenic views and hipster coffee shops. Maybe I would enjoy the scenery and watch the event take place from the stands.

Under further evaluation the next day, we all agreed I had strained or torn my hamstring. My doctors and coaches thought we would take it day by day until I got back to the U.S. to get imaging. My next stop was the U.S. Open where our orthopedic doctors were based, so I knew I would have answers soon enough. Until then, if I could bear the pain, I could ride. So, I rode.

I thought I would keep it simple for the event—warm up my leg and see if I could even get it moving. I was just doing straight airs through to warm up and it felt okay. I tried a basic run and it went okay, so I built and progressed slowly. That is until I landed on my first straight air of my third run and my whole leg seized. My hamstring locked up, and as I landed on the wall, I had no support. I kept falling right to the ground. I lay on my side in the flat bottom with the ESPN follow camera in my face for my close-up. With a burning pain in my leg, I picked myself up again and went to the doctor at the bottom. He immediately rushed me into the training tent.

Tears came again, a mix of frustration and months of disappointment, but again my body started to relax; the pain started to go away. The medical staff at the event and my personal team doctors concurred that if I could bear the pain I could try it out. I went back run by run and my leg started to work. It was time for the event—another X Games final.

I gritted out the first two runs, attaining third place with my safe, basic, qualifying run. I had one run left and, if I was going to make something happen, it had to be now. I was going to try a 1080, the 1080 that I had not landed yet, the 1080 that I would later find out tore part of my hamstring off the bone. It made for the best run all season. I bumped into second place and somehow was still walking. I was relieved and grateful, but my journey had really only begun.

## HIP SURGERY

Upon arriving in Vail, I had my doctors visits booked in tandem with my practice schedule. I finished up the first day on the hill and then went in for my MRI. The night before qualifiers, I got the call from my doctor confirming our suspicion that I had a small hamstring tear. Additionally, I also had a labrum tear. The labrum is the rim of your hip joint. It is hard cartilage that helps your femur rotate in your hip joint. If that wasn't enough, the end of my femur had some flat spots on it that were also contributing to these tears and limited movement. Like any athlete my first question to the doctor was, "Can I compete this week? If I compete will I do more damage to my body?" He said no. I said, "Okay, I'll see what I can get done this week and we will go from there. I'll be smart and keep it simple, and see if I can at least finish my season out."

In the meantime, he laid out my options and gave me some things to consider about getting my body healthy and strong again. I started to wrap my head around it while trying to stay focused on my event that week. I limped my way onto one last podium, landing in the third spot at my eightteenth U.S. Open. I have won that event more than anyone in its long history, it is my favorite and biggest event of the season. Any other event, I might not have pushed to see if I could fight through the pain to make something happen.

As I watched the men's final from the bottom of the halfpipe that day, I discussed my options with my doctor. We sent my imaging to the hip specialist, and, upon review, he recommended surgery. I talked to my team doctor, who knows what I demand from my body and what I want to accomplish in the next few years. I was walked through what the healing process and outcome would be. By the time the men finished competing, I had decided surgery was going to be the next event on my schedule.

My snowboard season came to an abrupt halt and my recovery season began. I left the U.S. Open the next day, and after a few days at home I went back to Vail for surgery. One of the perks of being an Olympian is that I have access to the best doctors in the United States, and they do their best to fit me in quickly. When I returned, the surgery went well. I stayed the night in the hospital only to be up on the bike the next morning at seven. There was no feeling sorry for myself, only a season shift that would hopefully put me back in competition shape.

## A NEW SEASON

The healing process started, but I was far from being able to take care of myself. Because of the cartilage repair, I had a lot of restrictions out of surgery. I could not sit at 90-degrees for the first three weeks. I spent eight hours a day in a CPM (Continuous Passive Motion) machine, four weeks in calf pumps whenever stationary to prevent blood clots, and every moment I was not in my machines I had to have my legs tied together so I would not externally rotate my foot and damage the area that was repaired. For the first four weeks I was completely dependent. I could not even get out of bed by myself, so if I had to go to the bathroom in the middle of the night I had to call someone to come help me out of my machines and out of bed. My amazing caretakers (my brother "Mr. Mom," sister-in-law and some of my best friends) joked about how I was like a puppy, "No water past 8:00 pm," they said, that way I would not wake everyone up at night for a bathroom break.

> *"I have learned that what doesn't*
> *kill you will make you humble."*

To say it was challenging is an understatement. People may think that competing is the hard part of an athlete's life; this experience led me to believe that recovering from injuries may actually be the most difficult part. My life came to a grinding halt and all of a sudden I was having to depend on others. It was the hardest challenge for this independent, strong achiever. I have learned that what doesn't kill you will make you humble.

Success for me was suddenly found in the simple things of life. Success was being able to take a shower on my own or making it from the car to physical therapy without needing to take a rest. If I flashed back a week previous, success was getting up on the podium at the U.S. Open. Now success was boiled down to life's basic functions, and I was faced with my limitations and reevaluating my expectations of myself.

Success can and will look different in different seasons. We have to know what season we are in and constantly be evaluating what success looks like. We all have seasons where success isn't about medals and victories but about growing and getting healthy. As I began recovery, I had to look at it with a big-picture perspective to see that ultimately this part of my process should eventually help me win medals again. If I refuse to embrace what success looks like in this recovery season, then I will never see the big-picture success that I am inevitably working toward. Success for me was being redefined. I had to start at the very beginning.

## REFLECTION QUESTIONS

*How has an unexpected obstacle changed your life?*

*What did dealing with adversity bring to the surface?*

*How do you define success in your current season?*

*2016 US Open - Vail, Colorado*

# CHAPTER SIX
# REDEFINING SUCCESS

*"Success is moving from failure to failure without losing enthusiasm."*

*-Winston Churchill*

Success can be defined in so many ways. There are internal and external measures of personal success. It can be defined by a cultural group or by those closest to you; the list is extensive. Perhaps the type of success we are most familiar with are the ideas of success put upon us by others, the external measures that can often define us if we aren't paying attention, and where we need to begin the redefining.

As a professional athlete, my entire world revolves around external success in the eyes of other athletes, the media, sponsors, coaches, etc. It can be a list of accomplishments, often an Olympic gold medal tops that list. Upon meeting me, people often ask me, "So do you do the Olympics then? Have you ever placed?" People are trying to get their head around what I do, then they are trying to categorize me by whether I have been successful or not, and it isn't entirely a bad thing. It becomes an issue when I let other people's definition of success have more weight in my life than my personal definition of success. Then I will spend my life trying to accomplish something simply to make myself more comfortable in conversations and be accepted.

Growing up, I needed to show my parents that I could be successful as a professional snowboarder. The world of professional athletics is not always a sure and stable career choice. So, when I told my parents my plan, it took some give and take, as well as some mutual trust and belief to make it happen. Snowboarding was a new sport and no one could predict its future. It was far from established in mainstream America like we see it today. It was risky from an athletic standpoint and it was also risky because my whole career was hinging on whether or not I could prove that was successful. If I could not prove to be a success by the end of my first year out of high school, I was going to have to kiss it all goodbye and head for freshmen orientation at the local college.

After I won Olympic gold in Salt Lake City, the first words to my father were, "Does this mean I don't have to go to college? Am I a success?" Looking back now, it seems odd, but that was a huge motivator for me. I wanted to show my dad that I could be successful, because it meant I kept getting to do what I loved. External ideas of success, such as winning the gold medal or ranking high, are often a starting point for us on our journey of defining what success looks like.

If I gauge success by accomplishments and other people's ideas of success, I would quickly think I am a failure every time I do not meet my goals. If we allow other people's ideas of success to be our defining reason for doing things, we will live a life that is constantly coming up short and we will feel like a failure—even if we are not. We must be able to see how those in our lives perceive success, but we cannot be defined by their perceptions. Each category of people will bring different demands. Our goal as the views of others are applied to our lives is to remain constant and to remember that when we are trying to accomplish big dreams, people will be watching. So, let's define what that looks like in my life for an example.

## WHAT DOES SUCCESS LOOK LIKE TO MY SPONSORS?

Everybody works for someone, even athletes. Like any partnership, I work with my sponsors and lay out a list of things I hope to accomplish so they know what to expect from me before we "sign on the dotted line." This mutual discussion is so important because neither side wants expectations to become greater than reality. If your expectations are not communicated to yourself and those around you, you could set yourself up for a big letdown. Most employers who are unhappy with their employees find that they have unmet expectations. In many cases, these employees have looked good on paper but haven't produced the goods in real life; they have overpromised and underperformed. It works the same in athletics, except they have a win and loss record to assess us by.

---

*"Everybody works for someone, even athletes."*

---

In my world, it is a priority that I work with my sponsors and they know my goals. My sponsors are my employers in a way. Through ongoing relationship and experience with my track record, they know what to expect from me. I found, even in my recovery season, they were some of the most supportive people around me. I got constant emails from various sponsors, checking in and wishing me well in my healing process. They know that traditional success may not come from me in the next season, but they do know that my big picture goal looks like another Olympic run. They are counting on my faithfulness and resilience to make it through like every other obstacle I had faced before. I ease any discomfort by my good communication. Because of this, it is easy for all of us to champion my small victories in a recovery season.

It doesn't have to be anything major. For me it was simple, direct replies to their inquiries and encouragements. I would often answer their emails saying, "Today I noticed I limped less" or "I rode the bike outside today for the first time." These small victories are key moments to invite them into so they can see how I am stewarding their investment in me. It also provides me with personal accountability to keep going, and helps me to not take the small steps for granted and to celebrate my progress. If I fail to communicate, then I set us all up for huge disappointment.

Imagine if I did not communicate to any of my sponsors when I got injured. I figure it is the offseason and they don't have to know because I will be better before the new season begins and I don't want them to get scared and doubt me. What if all of a sudden, the new season is approaching and I am not ready to compete? What happens now? They would be expecting great things from me, and I would be unable to deliver. How disappointing. They would lose faith and trust in me, and I would most likely be breaching more than my contract with them; they would lose trust in me. Having good communication helps define what success looks like in all seasons of life.

## WHAT DOES SUCCESS LOOK LIKE TO OUR FRIENDS AND FAMILY?

My father is an important figure in my life; like many fathers, he instilled in me the importance of doing my best. He wasn't concerned about the outcome as long as I gave my full effort in the process. This instruction has stuck with me and shaped my outlook as an athlete. I still hear it on the other end of the phone when I call my parents after an event. After all the analyzing of my runs, facts of the results, and exchange of perceptions, my dad still says, "You did your best, and that is most important."

*"Success should look beyond the medals."*

I am thankful that was the mantra my dad relayed to me through all my endeavors growing up. What my family and friends think of as success should be one step closer to what my true definition of success actually is than the opinions of onlookers and strangers. Success should look beyond the medals and be defined more as my effort and growth as a person. I want to be surrounded by people who think I am successful regardless of how I perform and who celebrate my progress. This perspective helps separate my value from my performance, which is essential in the world of professional athletics. I don't ignore performance, but I choose not to let it own or define me.

## WHAT IS SUCCESS FOR ME?

Success is beyond performance. I don't think success should be dependent on accomplishments, although they are part of the equation. Rather, it should be tethered to your growth and stewardship of your opportunities. At the end of the day, success needs to be *inspired* by the Olympic-sized dream but *defined* by things that are within your ability to control. Success should be distanced from comparison with others and united with the inner motivation to find your best self.

We are all at different points in our lives, careers and endeavors. Some people are considering retiring while others are dreaming of what they will one day be doing. We may be at different points in our understanding of success and even our path to it. I can respect that as I have been growing in my understanding of success throughout my whole career and seen new challenges and new victories at each stage. Perhaps it will have an ever-evolving definition for me.

## GROWTH AND CHANGE

Much like any kid would tell you, I used to think that success simply meant winning. Some people define success that way and stay with it their whole lives. We hear phrases like, "If you're not first, you're last!" and, "Winning isn't everything; it's the only thing." These ideologies filter through our minds and beg us to believe that "second place is the first loser." We often believe it.

I was watching the Summer Olympics in Rio, which is an interesting undertaking as a fellow Olympian. Watching the dynamics surrounding the Olympics from the outside provides a good reminder of what really matters. As each event took place, I was keenly aware that anything less than a gold medal equals disappointment. The greatest athletes in the world perform on the world's stage only to hear the commentator say, "A bronze medal is not what that athlete was looking for." It made my stomach turn.

Popular culture tells us over and over again that we only want winners. As the medal count flashes up on the screen every so often so we can measure ourselves against the rest of the world and pat ourselves on the back, we sigh a little when an athlete gets a silver instead of a gold. I can't help but think of all the other stories we never hear about—the stories of triumph and victory that have nothing to do with the podium. How did we get here?

I lived in that reality for many years. I have been the celebrated champion who was quickly forgotten the next week. Amongst the storm of information and the "next best thing" mentality that the world of sports has, every person is replaceable when they are no longer a winner. As challenging as it was to process this reality, it was probably the best thing that has happened to me. Understanding that winning isn't everything caused me to learn to define success as more than a place or a medal. I learned that it is more than an achievement, and if I am truly winning in the game of life, then I am finding fulfillment in who I am no matter how I do.

## WINNING ISN'T FULFILLMENT

My whole life I strived to be successful. I did not know what that looked like until I found this thing called snowboarding. Snowboarding was my ticket. I have been wildly successful, but the more I won, the more I discovered that success did not equal fulfillment. Winning and getting attention made me want to win more in order to keep people's affection. I was finally successful, but why was I not fulfilled? That was the question I found myself asking. I was at a loss for understanding after my first Olympic medal.

*"We often mistake success for significance."*

I had this idea that once you are successful you are fulfilled. Looking back now, I can see I was looking for something more than success; I was looking for significance. We often mistake success for significance. Our culture will tell us that success is the thing that we need the most. I would like to propose that it is not success that we most need but significance. Our greatest human need is significance and, until we can separate our significance from our performance, it is impossible to have lasting, fulfilling success.

## 2006: FINDING MYSELF

In the 2006 Winter Games I was not successful according to the medal count. I placed fourth and did not get a medal. A few years later, one of my dearest friends made this comment about my 2006 Olympic performance, "Getting fourth place in the Olympics was the best thing that ever happened to you because it caused you to figure out what you wanted." Her opinion is 100 percent true. That "loss" changed my life. When I left those Olympic games, I realized what I wanted, and I was

*"My growing love for my sport is directly linked to my identity and my ideas of success: fulfillment and, ultimately, significance."*

actually thankful because it helped me realize who I am. It is hard to be successful without knowing who you are outside of who people say you are or expect you to be. Through not living up to expectations and not achieving success I started to define what success looked like for me and realized that there was much more to it than just winning.

Don't get me wrong, I am all for going after your goals. I have dozens of them that I am still pursuing with everything in me. It is key, though, that we pursue them with a healthy sense of significance that is not dependent on our performance. If we can fail, miss the mark, have a setback, and still be okay with ourselves at the end of the day, then we know we are on the right track. Only then are we freed up to enjoy the pursuit of our dreams. If our self-view depends on how we perform, it is only a hop, skip and a jump to burnout, depression, anxiety, and a whole load of problems. It is an unrealistic expectation to think that you will always win or always be the best. Eventually those expectations will not be met, and unmet expectations lead to the worst version of yourself.

I think having a good grip on my identity outside of my ability to perform has helped me have a long, consistent, enjoyable snowboarding career. If burnout was linked to too much activity, I should be hot and crispy by now. I have done more snowboarding events than perhaps anyone on the planet, and I love snowboarding more today than I ever have. There are many times when I felt disappointment, frustration, and even times where I considered pursuing other things, but I kept myself anchored in who I am, and I was able to be passionate and define what I am alive to do. My growing love for my sport is directly linked to my identity and my ideas of success: fulfillment and, ultimately, significance.

## MY NEW DEFINITION

Once I started to figure out who I was apart from what I did, I was able to go after my dreams in a way I never thought possible. I was able to dream bigger than I ever had. When your self-worth is not tied to your winning or losing, you can take bigger risks than you ever considered, because, if you dream big and fail, you simply learn a way not to do it the next time. You still exist in that space; no one takes your place. As simple as it sounds, you can fall down and get back up. No harm, no foul. In taking bigger risks in this manner, I became more successful than I ever thought I could be.

If success is not defined by performance, then how is it defined? Success looks like intentional growth and progress. It looks like seeing where you are, seeing where you want to be, and making a plan to get there. I still have the same lofty goals to achieve that I did before I discovered who I am, but now I enjoy the process of getting to them. My focus is more on the journey than the destination. I set my eyes on the little wins and notice my growth along the way; the more I grow, the more I find that my idea of success has a lot to do with actually enjoying what I do. I think success is also marked by joy, or enjoyment. If you are growing and moving toward the goal while having fun, then you have cracked the code.

From a young age, we get asked, "If you could do anything you want and money were no object, what would it be?" Well, I want that answer to be exactly what I am doing with my life. I want to dream big, go after my passions, and love what I do. If we can allow our perspective to go beyond just achieving things, we can see the victories along the way, no matter how seemingly small. I have learned to love the process and be thankful for my opportunities.

There is a tension though; I would be lying if I said I love every day I am out on the hill. Have you ever been to Colorado in the winter? Some of our training days are in the negative double digits and—let's be real— no one enjoys those days. There is something to be said for gritting it out, which is how we get through those days—that and a lot of layers. Ultimately, we should be enjoying the process.

## DEFINING SUCCESS IN YOUR CURRENT PROCESS

As I type out these words, I am dreaming about my fifth Olympic games even though I am not even medically cleared to be on my snowboard. Some of you will read this book long after the 2018 Olympics are done and already know how I did. It is a strange thought. As I dream though, I understand that I am in a season of hard work and endurance. Right now, success, for me, looks like walking pain-free and getting out on the hill again. I am faithfully putting one foot in front of the other and celebrating one six-inch box jump at a time. That is success for me right now.

As I think about what I want to accomplish in my career, that fifth Olympics is on the horizon for me, and it is in my heart to go. So, what is success? Is it just going? Is it winning? How do I get there? If I went again and did not win, would that still be success? These things have to be considered. I have to know those answers and what my plan is to get there or I will lose my way when all the noise gets loud.

The Olympics for me are like little benchmarks every four years in my career. I have not always done it well, and I have lots of areas to learn and to grow in, but what I am most looking forward to is going through another Olympic cycle to seeing what tools I have picked up in the process that will help me hit my potential. Yes, when I get asked what my goals are, they are always the same: win Olympic gold. I have the same goal, but how I get there may be a little different, and I hope to be able to enjoy the process. Enjoying the process and seeing my progress are success for me.

## SUCCESS IS MORE THAN ACCOMPLISHMENTS

Success is more than accomplishments. On some level, we have heard that before, but I am not sure we adhere to it. Partly, I think it is because we don't often arrive at that so-called big accomplishment. If we were to interview people who have accomplished big things, we would quickly hear that it was not everything they thought it would be.

*"It is what goes on inside of us that really defines the value of those accomplishments and makes them fulfilling."*

As I look back at my career, I have the luxury of perspective. I can truly say that the victories that matter most to me are not the lofty external goals I set. When I recall the times that I rose to the occasion, regardless of what was going on in or around me, or the times that I put down a run against all odds to come in second or even third, and a number of other experiences, I am reminded to keep perspective. This sounds like something a well-meaning parent would say, "Just do your best, honey," but from the proper perspective, our best is enough and often more fulfilling than all the gold medals in the world. The truth is, after a while they are just more medals, but it is what goes on inside of us that really defines the value of those accomplishments and makes them fulfilling. It is by them that we can really measure if we were successful or not.

## REFLECTION QUESTIONS

*How can I tell how I define success?*

*How does outward success change you?*

*What if I become successful but my life still feels empty?*

*How do I face my definitions of success and redefine them?*

2012 – Snowpark, New Zealand

# CHAPTER SEVEN
# A NEW NORMAL

*"Dreaming, after all, is a form of planning."*
*- Gloria Steinem*

We spent an entire chapter defining success for a reason. You *must* know what success looks like to you. It needs to be written out, dreamed about, and made as specific as possible. There are blanket goals that seem intuitive, such as, every competitive pro snowboarder's goal is to win the Olympics. While that may be true, if you keep it so broad and it does not happen, then you will not be able to see what you actually did achieve along the way. Your unmet expectations will cause major disappointment. Defining personal success is maybe the most import thing you can do.

Define what your own personal success story looks like. What will you look back on and be proud of, inspired by, and at peace with? What would make your heart happy? That is a question I often ask myself. Your success has to be driven from what goes on in you, not by what goes on around you.

Defining that success is also helpful if you are not good at dreaming. Sometimes it is hard to define what it is that you want to do or achieve.

> *"Your success has to be driven from what goes on in you, not by what goes on around you."*

It can be even more difficult because society constantly champions visionaries, dreamers, and go-getters and doesn't always celebrate the people who do small things in a great way. If you are wired like the latter, it is easy to compare yourself to others and convince yourself of lies such as, "I'll never do anything great." Well, the truth is that what success looks like for someone else is not what success looks like for you. That is why it is so important to define it individually. If you don't, then you will constantly consume and work for something that is unobtainable. Success that is built on achievement, while externally tempting, is often hollow.

You must combat this comparison; comparison is a killer. Comparison steals from you and leads to all sorts of insecurity. If you are able to define what success looks like for you, you will not be offended when others are promoted or achieve greater things than you. Let me be the first to tell you: that can and will happen many times on your journey to your dream. If you don't define your success, everyone else will do it for you and you will spend your life comparing your level of success to the success of others.

## MAKING A SUCCESS PLAN

Once you have learned how to define or redefine success for yourself, it is time to make a plan. When dreaming on a large scale, it is important that you don't bite off more than you can chew. If you try to accomplish too much too fast, you could get discouraged. Remember, small victories lead to big ones. You should have measurable, small goals and refuse to allow yourself to get caught up in the one major thing that happens years down the road. I started snowboarding when I was just a kid, and even in my thirties, I have not accomplished the things that were in my heart 20 years ago. It is fuel for the fire of my motivation, not water to put it out.

Sometimes the one big goal at the end can overshadow the many small achievements that are equally important and necessary. With each completed small goal, we gain strength and courage. The feeling of belief in yourself pushes you to go further and farther. These milestones need to be set out specifically so they can be marked and celebrated. The reality is that no big achievement happens by accident. As we discussed earlier, just riding your potential will only get you so far, and it is the preparation and achievements along the way that get us ready for those big moments. So where do you start?

*"No big achievement happens by accident."*

## DESIGN WITH THE END IN MIND

Many great leadership books will tell you how important this is. It is something I read about in a John Maxwell book many years ago and has shaped every plan I make for my life. I start by figuring out where I want to go, then I work my way backward. It makes the big-picture goals more obtainable as I break it down into definable steps. You can dream the big dreams, as long as you define what it looks like for you to get there in small, measurable increments.

In Sochi, I was the gold-medal favorite. I came home with a bronze and it was one of my greatest achievements. People ask if I plan on winning gold when I go to the 2018 Olympics, and I always reply with, "That's the plan. That is always the plan." I always have that end goal, but that end goal does not define success for me; it is merely part of the plan. It is easy to get those mixed up. As I entered into training, I built my plan with this in mind. If you can't define the smaller steps, then you should reevaluate the goal. Be as specific as possible.

## MAKE YOUR GOALS MEASURABLE

Being able to see what you have done will keep your mind off of what you have not done yet. My friend Eric Johnson tells a story about measuring growth that has stuck with me. As with most families, they had a doorframe in their home where the heights of everyone in the family were measured. Everyone would stand their straightest and see if they grew since the last time they measured. As the years went on, this became really fun for his girls because they were noticing the change from one measurement to the next. At one phase, one of his kids asked to be measured every day. In his fatherly way, Eric had to explain to her that she had not visibly grown since yesterday. He concluded that it is not good to measure growth over short periods of time. Growth takes time; it cannot be measured in moments but in seasons. It is exciting, but we should not become so fixated on it that we are more discouraged by it than encouraged. If we look for growth too often, we won't be able to see the big gains we have actually made.

*"Growth takes time; it cannot be measured in moments but in seasons."*

I actually set goals every day that I am riding the halfpipe. If on a training day my goal for that day is to work on my 1080s, I cannot have that be my plan. It is a great goal, but how do I get there?

It starts with the small goals within the daily goal being marked out. I have to break it all down, one run at a time. I start with warm-up runs, then do some semi-final runs that are not as difficult but will get my timing firing. Finally, I move into the bigger tricks and spins. The more specific I am, the more beneficial it is for my training.

I actually count them. I do one straight air run, then I have to do my basic qualifier run three times. Once I have those solid, I move on to my main goal for the day, the 1080. Doing that helps me stay on track, and even if I do not get to the point where I am landing good 1080s, then at least I am doing good straight airs and good basic runs. Setting small goals on the way to a big goal helps you feel good in the process and good about your day even if the big goal does not come together that day.

## MAKE YOUR GOALS WITHIN THE REALM OF THINGS YOU CONTROL

That may sound like a no-brainer, but if you make your goals about something or someone other than you, then you will not be responsible for seeing them through to completion. You will be tempted to let yourself off the hook when things get hard. You open yourself up to the "blame game." It might seem odd, but the blame game is very common amongst competitive athletes. Everyone is looking for a reason, an excuse, for why they didn't win. In my sport, it is easy: "The pipe was not built correctly and the weather was terrible," or "The judges did not score me fairly." In other sports, it could be, "The ref was against us," "The other team's attitude threw me off," or even something as simple as, "It must be what I ate for breakfast." The list could go on forever.

If you give into this game even a handful of times, you will find it very difficult to get out of it. It is a devastating cycle of blame that causes many people to lose their drive and spend their lives telling everyone how great they could have been if it weren't for… something. You cannot be shifted by external factors. Only you get to decide what will affect you internally, and in the times where you are feeling sick or the weather is bad, you get excited about an opportunity to do your best in spite of the situation. At worst, you grow your belief in yourself. You begin to see how you are impacting your world instead of being impacted by it.

I have seen this play out even on the Olympic level. Entire news stories have been written about how something was wrong with the conditions of the halfpipe. While it can be true, it reveals someone who did not want to be responsible for how things turned out. If you can get this one down, you will happen to the world around you instead of having it happen to you.

## FAITHFULNESS AND ACCOUNTABILITY

I am successful when I look back at my process and see that I managed myself well, took advantage of opportunities, stuck to the plan regardless of what was going on around me, worked hard, and took risks when necessary. In short, I was faithful with what I was given. I want to reach the end of my career knowing that I made the most of what I had. It's not complex, it's not specific, but that idea can be applied to many different goals and dreams. It puts the responsibility on me, it is measurable, and it has the end in mind. I can't control the outcome, but I can do my part. I can choose to be faithful and put accountability to my process in my plan in order to achieve it. Accountability, letting people in to cheer you on and help you steward your dreams, is an element of the process you cannot ignore.

> *"I have people in it with me to pick me back up when I don't feel like getting up again."*

I will say it over and over again: behind every great athlete is a team of great people. We all need to get people in our corner. When you share your goals with people, it not only keeps you accountable, but it makes it more fun. As the professional athlete, I am the "front man," the person people see on television. But I can honestly say that I would not be there if it were not for constant investments from other people. My victories do not remain my own. I get to share them with other people. In the same manner, perhaps more importantly, when I fail, my failure is not my own; I have people in it with me to pick me back up when I don't feel like getting up again. They remind me who I am and call me higher to meet all the goals and make the most of my potential.

## WHAT DOES MY SUPPORT SYSTEM LOOK LIKE?

I have developed a structure around me to make me as successful as possible. It works well and when I find things that aren't working, I can adjust the system as I progress and my vision and goals change. It starts off with family and close friends and I build it out from there. No matter where I am in the world, my friends and family are only a text or call away thanks to technology.

## PEOPLE ON THE ROAD

I have quality people on the road with me. There are my teammates, coaches, physical therapists, sports psychologist, and my sponsors' support staff. It takes some practice and some self-evaluation to determine who to let onto this team. When I am nervous because I fell first run in the contest, I probably should not text my mom for support then—she would jump in and be nervous with me—but rather I should find someone in my circle who I know can pull me out of that nervous headspace. In that situation, my coach would be a good bet for appropriate advice and motivation. My coaches know me, and we have a barrage of inside jokes; with just one mention of one I can already be laughing and getting my emotions to a place that will help me achieve what I set out to do. It can be as simple as that.

I also work on the practical side of things by communicating my end goals and personal benchmarks to all of my on-hand staff before the season starts. I talk to my coaches about tricks I want to learn and put target dates for those so I can be ready for the next Olympic cycle. I talk to my sports psych about what I am struggling with, and she reminds me of what I have overcome in the past and who I am. I work with my trainers on how my body is feeling and we make a strategy. To my on-hill staff during the events, I also communicate what I need and what success looks like for me beyond the apparent goal each day. This should be a trusted circle, or "circle of trust" if you will. I trust these people's judgment in tandem with my own. I can't tell you how many times I pulled on these people and went with what they said to do rather than how I was feeling at the time. I am successful because I take feedback and remain teachable. Those things are essential in the process of life. If you can do those two things, you will be more successful than you ever could be on your own.

Find your support group and do life with them so that, in the highs and lows of the journey, they can jump in and help you along the way. I love the description of encouragement that I have heard: "People put courage in us, and it goes from the word 'encouragement' to 'in-couragement'." That is what your support system should do; they should be the people who put courage in you.

## FRIENDS WHO ARE PRESENT

In addition to that first line of defense or offense, however you see it, I personally feel supported when I have people at my events. As many of my peers and people I grew up snowboarding with have retired, I know I need friends along the journey and make sure I have a friend at most of my events. These friends need to like you for who you are, not what you do. That is probably the most important aspect of a support person. Find people who are looking to give instead of get. They can stay constant as my friend no matter what my performance.

## FRIENDS FROM AFAR

I write email updates to about 50 of my extended friends during every event. I update them on how I am doing, what I am struggling with, what I want to accomplish; and I ask for their encouragement and prayer support. It is a great way for me to stay connected with people while I am on the road, and I love the support and encouragement I get from the emails that come back.

Potential will only get you so far. Take that potential and build a foundation to stand on. It is people who have put both potential and faithfulness to work for them who meet their fullest potential. Surround yourself with people who believe in you for the days when you don't believe in yourself. Please remember, behind every great athlete is a team of great people. Identify what you can control and design with the end in mind.

## REFLECTION QUESTIONS

*How do you measure success?*

*What does your support system look like?*

*What small things can you start doing in a great way?*

*2008 - Mount Cook, New Zealand*

# CHAPTER EIGHT
# FEAR OF WHAT?

*"You gain strength, courage, and confidence by every experience in which you really stop to look fear in the face. You must do the thing which you think you cannot do."*

*–Eleanor Roosevelt*

Sometimes you can do everything right and it still goes terribly wrong. No amount of goal-setting or preparation will prepare you for every variable. There are so many aspects of snowboarding that cannot be perfectly calculated. You can have all your goals mapped out, prepared to the best of your ability, and everything lines up with the team, and even then, success is not guaranteed. Heading into the Vancouver Olympics no one was more ready than me.

In the four years prior to Vancouver, I made sure I was prepared and ready for anything. In reality, I waited eight years to get back up on the Olympic podium; I worked to give myself the best possible chance of winning.

There is a lot of media focus around the Olympics but, up until the

Opening ceremonies kick things off, there is not a lot of content to report on apart from how the venues are coming along. The mainstream media talks about how the host cities did or did not prepare enough. They talk about if they will get the Olympic village done in the allowed time before the athletes start arriving, and they traditionally discuss the weather and report on the courses that are coming together. As an athlete, I have learned that I cannot pay too much attention to these reports. I know there are only so many things I can control, so getting hung up on things I cannot control is not going to contribute to a good performance.

That early winter in 2009-2010, there was, however, one story that started to stand out—it was warm, very warm. You think to yourself, *It's still December; winter is just getting started. They must still have time to build the Pipe; surely they can still get it done.* What started as "just a story" quickly turned to a concern in early February when the weather hadn't changed much. While I hoped they would figure it out, I couldn't help but search the Internet for photos. As a competitor, I should have been focusing on getting my runs perfected so I would be polished before the Olympic flame got lit, but I found, much to my disappointment, the reports were true; there was no snow for the halfpipe.

The snowboard events for the 2010 Winter Olympics were to be hosted at a small resort just outside of Vancouver called Cypress, while many of the Alpine events were being held at Whistler Blackcomb Resort. Whistler was a few hours north of the city where it was typically snowier and much colder, while Cypress was nearly at sea level.

At training camp, I was sitting in the house with other Team USA Olympians watching online as venue builders tried desperately to gather enough snow to build the halfpipe in time. After many desperate attempts, they decided to build it out of bales of hay—that's right: hay bales. Here's how it worked. The builders would make the bulk of the wall out of hay and then cover it with snow. Where was that snow coming from since none was falling on-site? It was being brought in from the nearby mountains by helicopter. Yes, we were stunned for words. Many times we asked, "They cannot be serious. The Olympic halfpipe will be made out of hay?"

As the situation unfolded, I reminded myself that I had spent my lifetime as an athlete getting ready for this, to be at my pinnacle of performance. Even as I was watching the stuff of nightmares play out before me on the nightly news, I was thinking through ways to adapt. I say nightmare because it was scary. I was a little afraid to be honest, but as with disappointment, it is okay to encounter it from time to time. Problems happen only when you stay there and partner with them. It would have been a lot easier if the situation improved.

---

*"If we look for bad news, we will surely find it."*

---

Unfortunately, it didn't end there. The workers soon found out after they covered the hay in snow that the walls were so unstable that it would be dangerous to have a crowd standing on it. The few people walking on the walls were causing the bales to separate, so they canceled all the tickets for wall viewing for the halfpipe event. It was not safe for walking, but all good to have an Olympic event on them… It was a very difficult situation that we were in.

In this situation, and in life, there seems to be no shortage of bad news available to us. Is it all really bad news or are the bad things just stealing the show? It is true with news, as with every life situation: you will find what you look for. No matter what the circumstance, you need to be looking for the opportunity found in various difficult situations. In situations where past experiences want to tell us that there is no hope, there is no good way out, we need to always believe and always hope that we can overcome. We need to evaluate what we are looking for and what we are hoping in; it is in that place that opinions are formed and the lens that we look through gets developed. If we look for bad news, we will surely find it. Likewise, if you look for the opportunity, you will find one.

As the nightmare continued, I was prepared all the same. Every bad-weather day and every train wreck of a halfpipe I had ridden the previous four years made me ready for this, and I wasn't going to focus on the bad. This problem affected every competitor in the event, so I had to stay focused. If I could steer clear of the complaining and the chatter around the unfortunate events, I could still do my best. That's what I believed anyway as I was packing my bags and heading for my third Olympics.

I was optimistic in spite of the bad report. When I arrived, I found it is much more difficult to be "glass half full" after you arrive and see that the glass is completely empty. The Pipe was bad—the worst Pipe I had ever seen. We were originally supposed to have five practice days, but they were cut down to three days. "Days" was a relative term because those "days" were sometimes limited to three runs per person, as to not put too much wear and tear on the soft and melting halfpipe. It was an opportunity to face fear and refuse to be discouraged or jump on the bandwagon of blame.

The only good thing to look forward to was that the finals were at night. Maybe, just maybe, the evening event would keep the temperature cooler so we could have an Olympic event that allowed for each competitor's best runs. The event began.

I made it through qualifiers and was ready for the finals. Despite everything, it was actually going okay. I was not riding at my best, but I was seeded first heading into finals, so I still had a chance. Sometimes it is not about having the best run you have ever done; it is about having the best run that day. That was a real possibility for me—one I was desperately hoping I could pull off.

The sun went down and finals were about to start. I had two runs, two opportunities. My first run was going well as I wound up for my last hit. The snow was soft and bumpy, so it was easy to dig my edge in and go straighter than I wanted. My last hit I got forward and went too straight. When you hit a twenty-two-foot wall at full speed and don't put any downhill angle on, it kicks you off of it pretty quick, and I got kicked right into the flats. I did a front-side 900 into the flat. I tried to keep it together, but my arm and my butt slammed into the slushy bumpy flat bottom. Before I knew it, my first run was over and I was left with a throb in my right wrist and a flood of memories from 2006.

As I flashed back to 2006, I thought about the trick that kept me off the podium: a front-side 900 on the last hit into the flats. It was like a bad movie playing over and over again—except it was real life. It was my biggest fear playing out in front of me on the world's biggest stage. I am not sure what could have been worse.

I went to the top and, as is tradition in situations like this, I said, "What an opportunity..." to my coaches, and they echoed it back to me. I also went and got my wrist looked at and the trainer said, "Just keep moving it," which is code for, "It's most likely broken but we don't want to freak you out before your final run." Regardless, I dropped in for one more run and went for it. When I got to that big moment, the last hit, my biggest fear, I landed it. I landed it and rode out good enough to capture an Olympic bronze.

It was not gold, it was not silver, but it was victory for me. It was victory in that I faced my biggest fear and won. It was more than winning a medal. I knew what I had faced that day and I knew that I overcame the worst-case scenario and my biggest fear simply by persevering. I looked fear in the face and walked away triumphant.

## FACING FEAR

Fear is a universal human emotion; it comes in many forms. Sometimes it is big and dramatic and you are terrorized by the enormity of the

---

*"We often have to overcome our*
*greatest defeat to find true victory."*

---

situation, but not all situations are that obvious. Fear is also subtle. It invites you to partner with it over time, and slowly by slowly you end up in the trap that is hard to get out of unless you are intentional. You see, I had chosen a relentless outlook before I needed to be relentless. I knew that I would have the chance to partner with fear at some point during the Olympics. Because I was prepared, I was able to keep it together when I faced the very thing that tore me down the previous Olympics.

We often have to overcome our greatest defeat to find true victory. In the rarest form, it will come to light with a reward or a medal. Most of the time, it is only an individual who knows the true depth of the victory they won. Internal victories are just as important as external ones.

When people discover I snowboard professionally, one of the first remarks I get is, "That is crazy!" or "You must be so brave!" Their response is not abnormal; in fact, people often negatively label others they don't understand or relate too. We often cannot relate because we have no grid for the experience and if we were put in their shoes we would be terrified. People look at what I do on my snowboard and think, "That is scary." Looking at it from a practical level, they are right. They see scary, insane, even reckless risk, but I know it is a calculated risk. What is scary to me is not scary to other people. I would be terrified if I had to fly a plane. Why? Well, because I don't know the first thing about flying planes. My fear is based on my lack of information. Information and preparation are great antidotes to fear.

It is a very fine line to walk as a snowboarder and as a human. We want to stay within our ability level, but on the other side of our ability level is the fear level—a place we have to enter if we want to grow ourselves and compete in an ever-changing world. I want to get better and push

> *"Once you agree with fear, it has the tendency to consume you."*

it, but when I don't know what I am doing or how to do it I can quickly befriend fear. When fear becomes familiar, your mind can race to all sorts of places that you do not want to go. Once you agree with fear, it has the tendency to consume you. It has an addictive trait to it that is almost paralyzing. It sneaks into thinking pretty convincing scenarios, and those scenarios are usually the worst-case ones.

## THE FEAR FACTOR

People are at their worst when they are afraid. Have you ever seen or heard stories about people when they start to struggle in the water, when they feel like they are going to drown? The situation is very dangerous not just for the person drowning but for everyone around them. When a person comes to save them, quite often they try to drown the rescuer. Why? Because they are afraid; they are in fight or flight mode, and it clouds their judgment. Everything is distorted. Professional lifeguards are aware of this and plan the rescue to take away fear.

Maybe you never experienced what it feels like to drown, but you probably have found yourself in a dark room. In that space, every small thing, be it the creak of the floor or the tick of the heater turning on, makes your hair stand on end. You bump into something, and even though you know it's harmless, your mind goes straight to, "What was that? Who is here?" Something falls over, "It's wet!" Then someone comes in, turns the light on, and you realize you kicked over the dog's water bowl—no big deal.

Well, a minute ago your heart was racing and your imagination was going 100 miles a minute about all the scary things that were lurking in that dark room. Our imaginations can get us into trouble when partnered with fear. Imagination is a beautiful thing when partnered with hope, but when partnered with fear we become afraid of sharks in swimming pools. We all know that there is not a great white shark that appears in our swimming pool after we get in, but watch an evening of shark week and see how comfortable you are swimming in your six-foot deep swimming pool at night.

We can look to natural things like snowboarding or being an untrained pilot and say, "Sure, that is scary." We all have irrational thoughts from time to time; it's part of being human. Anxiety tells you, "I'm afraid right now and I don't know how I got here." A good number of us would say we are not fearful in our day-to-day life, but we have anxiety from time to time. It is something every person learns to navigate in his or her own way. We may not think anxiety is fear, but it is. For me, I feel fear when I am threatened. I have to learn to identify what that threat is and what triggers me. There are a number of things that cause fear in our lives. Identifying what makes us feel threatened is more than half the battle. Identifying that is like turning the light on in a dark room.

## FEAR OF FAILURE

Fear of failure says to you, "Nice try, but no matter how hard you try, you will never succeed." I check my heart in this area often as successes and failures are the measuring stick of my work place. I can tell pretty quickly how my heart is doing and where its significance lies if I take a minute to check in. If I have extremely high anxiety at an event, I usually start with this question: "What am I afraid of?" That is a simple and

*"If you spend all your time thinking about failing, failure is sure to be found."*

good tool to determine where your anxiety is coming from. It is often a small fear that, if exposed, is easy to side step. For me, it ends up being a fear that I won't do well today at the event or a narrative telling me how I am going to fail.

A practical way to combat the fear of failure is to find and celebrate small successes along the way. Ask yourself what you are doing right instead of what you are doing wrong. Being self-critical and constantly analyzing your failures will lead to more failure. It is the same principle about where you put your focus. When I go mountain biking, I know that if I don't want to hit the tree, I definitely don't want to look at it. If I want to stay on the path, I don't look directly at the ground beneath me, but I look down the path I want to take. By principle, if you spend all your time thinking about failing, failure is sure to be found.

> *"If your only definition of success is to win,*
> *then you will always be afraid to lose."*

Many people struggle with a fear of failure because their definition of success has to do with winning or losing. If your definition of success is requiring a definitive win and you compare yourself to someone who wins, then you isolate yourself from the rest of the process that gets you there. You cannot see the bigger picture of the small wins and progress you have made throughout the process. When you do this, there is no room for little victories; it becomes standing on the podium or nothing.

When I know that I am faced with the fear of failure, I goal set with the big goal of winning, but I also look to where I have little things to learn or gain or grow. We discussed goal setting in a previous chapter, but this is huge as you redefine success continually. I find success in my life when I have success defined by growth. If your only definition of success is to win, then you will always be afraid to lose. If your idea of success is to enjoy the process and grow, then you will never find a failure that you cannot overcome.

## FEAR OF INSIGNIFICANCE

The fear of insignificance has become a real issue for the "you can be anything you want to be" generation. Many people's biggest fear is that their life will end without ever accomplishing anything significant. The sad thing about that is that most of them probably had a desire and even the skillset to do something that mattered. Somewhere along the way though, they became so afraid that they wouldn't amount to anything that they didn't amount to anything. If you look for significance in your accomplishments, you will never really experience freedom in this area.

You cannot get your significance from what you do. When you are dreaming, it is easy to get wrapped up in the idea of the dream, the concept of it, and how people will treat you once you accomplish it. It is a normal thought process until it consumes you. I operated this way for many, many years; it stole so much from me.

Imagine if I got my sense of self-worth by how I placed in my competitions. If I won, all was right in the world. If I lost, all of a sudden I was a nobody. That sounds dramatic, but if we really examine the way we think, we will find it is not too farfetched. That sort of thinking would make things very intense and I would be in constant turmoil. We are at our worst when we live in fear. I would make things really difficult for me if I had the threat of my self-worth hanging in the balance in my mind right before every halfpipe run. What a challenging road that would be.

I remember my first X Games as the defending Olympic champion. The level of riding at the event was top-notch. My good friend Gretchen Bleiler was having the season that sent her into years of dominance in the competitive halfpipe world. I rode well that day and ended up in second place behind Gretchen. After the event, the media interviewed me in the finish area after my run. The microphone was thrust into my face and they said, "Disappointing final today, Kelly, what went wrong?" I had a moment of stunned silence on live television but eventually I came out with, "I was happy with my riding and my second place position and was so happy to see Gretchen do so well today." I walked away with the impression that if I did not win, I was a nobody. This is an extreme example, but it is what the world around us constantly communicates to us. It can be a challenge to be so counter-cultural in our thinking, but it is essential to our emotional health.

*"Significance is something you cannot get through accomplishment."*

It is one of the most challenging things to be consistent in because I do care about winning and bringing my absolute best to each event. My significance cannot be found in the place I stand in relation to the top of the podium. I have to keep myself in check and be self-aware enough to not tear someone else or myself down simply because I feel insignificant. In a culture that places performance above progress, your significance must come from who you are on the inside on days when no one is watching, the cameras are turned off, and you are living your life as you. It is normal to want significance.

In reality, one of our greatest needs as human beings is to find significance. We look for it all over the place. We search it out in relationships, families, accomplishments, and through performing. We think the need for unconditional love and acceptance can be met if we just marry this guy or get that job. Unfortunately, significance is something you cannot get through accomplishment, and we can't let it be defined by winning as we discussed in chapter six. It is something you have to work out apart from what you do. If you ever find yourself trying to arrive, there is a good chance you are trying to be defined by it. As my Olympic experiences went on throughout the years, I realized at each Games that I was defined less by being an Olympian and more by being me, Kelly Clark. This attitude freed me up to enjoy my sport at a higher level.

## FEAR THAT MOTIVATES

Imagine taking a walk through the woods on a peaceful afternoon. The breeze is blowing just enough to keep you cool and the sun is shielded by the trees. As you walk around the corner, out of nowhere a bear scurries out from behind a tree and rears up on his hind legs. You know you are in trouble now. What would you do? Why would you do it?

This is not a trick question. The answer is simple: run for your life! You would probably run faster than you ever have if a bear was chasing you. I know I would. You would run fast out of a reaction to fear. There is no fault in it, but it is definitely not fun and a very normal but reactionary way to approach situations. Doing this puts you at the mercy of fear. It can work and produce something in your life, but it is not sustainable or enjoyable. Also, for the record, you are not supposed to run from bears; you should back away slowly. Perhaps that is the better response we should have when we encounter things that scare us in our everyday life.

This may sound strange, but sometimes we think fear is okay if it is producing something good in our lives. Many companies and organizations try to motivate workers to do a better job with the fear of losing their positions. While this inflicts fear, perceived respect and hard work, it also paralyzes employees from performing at their full potential. This obedience does not lead to excellence, rather just enough to not get fired. You cannot hit your full potential if you are motivated by fear. If your goal is only to get the desired result at any cost, then the fear of not getting the result is motivating you—not love or passion or vision for something more. When this terrible tunnel vision narrows, you become so focused on just making it happen, you don't care if you enjoy it or even what lengths you will violate your core values to get it. It is a temporary stopgap, not a way of life. Stopgaps that become lifestyles are not sustainable and most definitely lead to the fear of insignificance and, ultimately, burnout.

Snowboarding events are a great example of this. I see people ride all year, and I know what tricks they do on the regular days that are not televised. Once we get into an event setting, people start to say things like, "Well, I guess I have to do my 9 now," or "Events are great because they force me to do my best tricks." Yes, the fear of not doing well can motivate, but as I stated before, it can produce results, but when we operate this way we will not hit our fullest potential, much less enjoy the process.

## FEAR OF LOSING CONTROL

Fear of losing control is something that high-level professionals face every single day. In my field, being in control of your body is extremely important, because mistakes can mean time off snow or even a hospital visit. On a regular day, if I managed myself well, or if I controlled myself well, it was a good day. It really is as simple as that. If I notice myself getting worked up over things I cannot control, it is easy to realign myself with what I can do. I start to do a routine, or talk to someone encouraging, anything to get my mind off of the fear that I am losing control.

As I have been processing the high level of preparation in my life, I realized that some of it can be rooted in control. For many years, everything about my life has been calculated and scheduled. Don't get me wrong, preparation is important; however, if preparation leads to a dependence on that preparation, it quickly becomes control. The problem with control is that it creates a fear of being out of control.

My all-time favorite movie is a movie about football called *Rudy*.

> *"There is always an element of mystery*
> *that requires trust and sometimes faith."*

Inspirational sports films are my go-to movies—weird, I know. There is an interaction between the main character, Rudy, and the priest who is helping get him into Notre Dame to play football. He made sure that he did everything he could to get accepted to the university, and their interaction went like this:

Rudy: "Is there anything more I can do? Have I prayed enough?"

"I'm sure that's not the problem," the priest replied

"Then how can I know that I've done everything?" Rudy probes.

The priest responds simply, "Son, in all my years of theological studies, I have come to the harsh conclusion that there are only two truths I know for sure: There is a God . . . I'm not Him."

Likewise, I find that with all my experience, understanding and planning, I am never in control. There is always an element of mystery that requires trust and sometimes faith. I am learning to let go of control so I can enjoy my life and progress. All of the preparation should be calculated but not to the point of control. If I am always afraid that I am going to not be in control, then I will be moved with every circumstance that isn't in the realm of my control. This mindset is detrimental to all progress in life.

## FEAR OF DISAPPOINTMENT

Disappointment is rooted in unmet expectations. Whether a fear of disappointing myself or disappointing others, there is a real identity struggle wrapped up in this fear. Most people's self-esteem and self-worth are not found in who they are but in what the most important person or group of people in their life think about them. Peer pressure and self-esteem aren't struggles you simply grow out of. People think once high school is over and you survive, then it just goes away. As most adults know, it continues and even increases as you get older. The higher the bar is set, the easier it is to let someone down.

In our society, disappointment is often accomplished through comparison. I work in an industry where social media is a major platform for athletes to make a name for themselves as celebrities apart from their performance on the hill. We begin to measure people's lives by their highlight reel of nicely posed snapshots, not paying attention to the everyday normal that they too get to live. Our level of access to information has increased and our access to the "amazing moments" of other people's lives without getting to see the vulnerable or painful ones can lead to false realities.

Ultimately, we need to be comfortable with who we are and where we are. The fear of disappointment lies to you and makes you think that you will always let someone else down. I want to be comfortable in my skin. I find it easy to compare myself with someone and forget that what success looks like to them is really different from what success looks like to me. Reminding yourself of what you are building is a good way to defuse this fear. If I see someone who is getting attention and sponsorships in my industry for something I would never do, I have to be okay with that. Even if I might disappoint my fans, coaches, or sponsors, I have to make sure I am not disappointing myself.

Freeing yourself from what people think about you is not a fun or easy process, but it is necessary. You may have to revisit it a few times in your life, as it always seems to creep back in on some level when pressure is added or a situation changes. Keep pushing, don't give up, and find the people who will celebrate you whether you are first place or last. These people will anchor you in the identity of someone who is accepted apart from their performance.

## COMPARISON WITH YOURSELF

If you are wired anything like me, then you are your toughest critic. Questions such as "Are you the best you at this moment?" constantly flood my mind; and a list of a time in life when I was fitter, less stressed, more focused, or more disciplined than I currently am is easily accessible. It may be true, but it is not a helpful thought process to moving forward in any area of life.

When I was eighteen years old, I could snowboard all day without stretching or warming up. I could ride seven or eight days in a row and never get tired. As you know, I am not eighteen, and that simply is not an option for me anymore. I simply don't have enough in the tank, and some days my tank seems like it has a large hole it in. I still have the same quality fuel, but it doesn't last as long as it once did, and it takes longer to refill it.

> *"I will always find myself lacking if I compare myself to a different me in a different time of life."*

I now know I am at my best when I am fresh and rested. I now train smarter, not harder. In my youth, it was the other way around. It would be silly to expect the same things I expected from myself back then. I have new routines and new strategies because this is a new season of life. I will always find myself lacking if I compare myself to a different me in a different time of life.

You must have the understanding that your past doesn't have to limit your future. As you celebrate what you did in the past, it can lead you to define what success looks like today. It's okay to look different from those around you. How I do things looks much different from how my competitors do things. They practice on all the training days leading up to an event, while I have to pick one of the three days to take off so I can have fresh legs for the contest day. I have to know myself and trust my process in that place. While more practice would benefit my competitors, it would destroy me. I have had to learn to let go of things like practice and conventional wisdom. Know yourself and your process; it may look different but it is important to accept it. If I was not open to adapting, changing, and reworking my process, I would have retired years ago.

As I've gotten older, I have gotten more comfortable in my own skin. In my mid-20s I thought I was comfortable, but now, in my early 30s, I am finding security in myself and getting rid of insecurities by accepting who I am now. We never arrive, but we get to keep growing and progressing.

## COMPARISON WITH OTHERS

When there is a dominant person in a sport, beating them becomes the goal. I went on a 16-win winning streak in the 2011-2012 season and I had a target on my back. If you looked at it, yes, naturally I was the one to beat. I would overhear the questions my competitors would get in interviews: "Kelly has not lost an event this season, do you approach things differently because of that?" "What is your strategy for beating Kelly?" I always find questions like that disrespectful to the person being interviewed for several reasons, but mainly because it took the focus off of their personal goals and put it onto me; beating me became the goal, not doing their best.

One of my friends made history at the X Games during the following 2013 season. She was the first woman to land a double in competition. It was historic, inspirational, and downright incredible. She was also the person who had snapped my win streak at the end of the previous year. People had turned our stories into a rivalry, and that became the new storyline. We knew what each other were capable of. She was planning on bringing it that night, and I knew I was going to have to stick to my strengths and land the best run I could dream up if I wanted to win. I did just that. I dropped into a 15-foot 1080 followed by a run that was as close to perfect as I have ever done. When her turn came, she did just what we all anticipated—she made history and showed us all what women are capable of.

When the scores came in and the comparison was done, I narrowly walked away with the win. Even though she did what no other woman had done, it was still not enough to win the event that night. Her achievement that day made history, but my win became the focus. Sometimes events can be a discouraging and frustrating experience because comparison overshadows people's individual victories.

> *"Comparison will rob you of things that are truly worth celebrating."*

Why? Because somewhere in the process people had turned the goal into her beating me again, and not for her to do her best. When we make the goal traditional types of success, we open ourselves up to disappointment even when we achieve some of our greatest moments. If we allow it, comparison will rob us of things that are truly worth celebrating. Comparison will rob us of real joy. I know this. I can write this out and understand it, but as with many things that have their root in fear, it is good to keep it on my radar. I have had to revisit this concept multiple times in my career to make sure my motives check out with my definition of success.

Comparison can sometimes push us to greatness, but when the idea of greatness becomes the goal instead of achieving our personal best, it can destroy us. My friend is one of the most courageous people I know and I love how she was able to stay true to herself in the midst of people's opinions. Her best that day was a milestone in our sport that will forever be remembered.

## DON'T LOSE FOCUS

Years ago, a sports psychologist came to work with our team and he demonstrated an important principle for us. He took two tennis balls and gave them to two of us. One person was to throw the ball up and down repeatedly while the other ball was to be thrown across the room. We were to keep a running count of the number of times each ball was thrown. As you might suspect, we could not keep the running tally accurate for both balls. We could only keep track of one thing at a time.

The concept of the experiment was to count tennis balls crossing a room and illustrate that you cannot focus on two different things at the same time. Many people blame mistakes and failures on the fact that they "lost focus," but many times it is because they tried to focus on too many different things at one time. If I am thinking about how hungry I am when I am about to drop in for a run, there is a good chance I am going to crash before the end of the run. Staying focused on what is in front of you right now will help dispel fear in any form.

Ultimately, fear steals joy. It operates undercover, so we need to identify it and see where it lies in our thinking so we can disarm it. We are supposed to dream dreams and then go after them and we should enjoy the process. Fulfilling a dream is not supposed to be some laborious task. We should enjoy the journey as much or more than the destination. I love the destination, but I welcome the process. That is the best way to grow and conquer fear in all forms.

## REFLECTION QUESTIONS

*What is your biggest fear?*

*How do you deal with comparison?*

*Are you defined by what you do?*

*How do you stay focused?*

2014 - Snowpark, New Zealand

# CHAPTER NINE
# THE REMODEL

*"Isn't it funny how day by day nothing changes,
but when you look back everything is different."*

*-C. S. Lewis*

My life often feels like a puzzle. I find myself wishing I could look at the puzzle box one more time to see where each and every color and odd-shaped thing should be placed. At the same time, if I had everything together I would miss out on that satisfaction of snapping each and every piece together. When things come together and you see the progress and growth in your life, the sometimes confusing and uncomfortable seasons of life become worth it.

I often look to the world around me to remind me how things work. Things seem to always be in motion even if we cannot see the motion and change at first glance. Just as the seasons in nature seem to tick by like clockwork, so do my own personal seasons and cycles of life. It is common for me to want to be in the harvest seasons of life, enjoying the fruits of my labor. I get to enjoy everything I have worked hard for and enjoy what has sprung up in my life. The reality is that seasons always change. To get back to the fruitful season where we can see the manifestation of things we have worked hard for requires a willingness to endure so we can bear more fruit.

One season is not better than another; they all have their purpose and are co-dependent. You can't have a harvest season if you have not planted in spring and tended to things in summer. It starts with knowing simple things, like what crops to plant in which season. A farmer knows down to the day when to plant and when to harvest. We must be able to do the same thing for the seasons of our lives. As Pastor Banning says, "It is impossible to thrive in life if you don't know what season you are in." So, what season are you in?

## THE DREAM

Last year I was spending my summer like I always spend it, in Wanaka, New Zealand. I have traveled to the southern hemisphere to train every August for the last ten years. It is one of my favorite trips, filled with snowboarding, friends, and good coffee. We had the usual mix of sunny bluebird days, "windy as" days (to use a Kiwi expression), and stormy down days for adventuring around the South Island; it was all routine for me until I went to sleep one night.

I don't often remember my dreams, so when I wake up and I am able to piece together the different elements, I take notice. Over the years, I have learned to pay attention to the dreams I remember because they always seem to end up being significant to me on some level. So, on this late winter night in New Zealand, when I awoke from a very vivid dream, I took note. After dismissing all the possible reasons for a vivid dream, like midnight pizza or an intense movie, I remembered I had not dreamt in months; this one could be significant to me. It was simple and clear, so I wrote it down.

In the dream, I was at my childhood home in Vermont, the place I associate with my formative years. I was watching the dream happen and was in it at the same time. It started with me in the back of the house on the outside staircase. I saw myself going up and down, up and down the stairs. I wanted to go inside but was unable to as there was no porch at the top of the stairs to get me to the door. I could not figure out how to get to the next level of the house, and right as I was feeling frustrated and was descending the stairs one last time, I had a thought: *I need to call the Master Builder to remodel so I can go to the next level.* At that moment, I woke up.

As I lay in bed contemplating the scene, I remembered something I heard on a podcast: "The reward for fruitfulness is pruning because it is your path to even greater fruitfulness." I thought to myself, *Remodel... pruning? Oh no.* I could see the value in such a process, but I was not sure I wanted to sign up for that—not at that time anyway. Things were going well; my life was simple and straightforward. I took note of everything in my journal and went about my day. I had decided to put it aside, but it did not put me aside.

We were scheduled to be on snow the next day, but a bad weather day intervened so I elected to go to a local winery with some friends who call Wanaka home. As we toured the vineyard and sat down to enjoy our meat and cheese plate, the winery's pooch came bounding up to me out of nowhere. The dog seemed to like me, but as I love dogs, it was fine with me. I thought I would throw its stick for it a few times. The vineyard workers came up shortly after and said, "Wow, he loves you. Our dog, Prune, really loves you." They kept saying his name, Prune, and it was then that the dream came rushing back to me. I thought to myself, *Your dog's name is Prune? Who names their dog Prune?* I was consumed with the dream all over again.

*"Often my head can get onboard before my heart."*

I began to assess the pieces of the dream and was getting my head around the idea of a remodel happening in my life. Often my head can get onboard before my heart, so I decided to think through it first. For me, as with many others, my head sets the plan and purpose in motion and my heart eventually lines up with it. I was getting my mindsets in order because I live by the understanding that mindsets are powerful things, and if we don't allow them to be malleable within the confines of our core value set, they can become a stumbling block to growth and change. Right as I was moving on and getting back to life in New Zealand, a swift and sudden season change came my way.

## AND SUDDENLY

Prior to traveling to New Zealand, my father was scheduled to have a serious yet routine back surgery. Because of the routine nature of it, I was not prepared for the conversation I would have with my family following the operation. Initially, I talked to my mom when he was out of surgery and in recovery—everything had gone to plan. Because it was about 9:00 am New Zealand time and bad weather had come in, we left the hill early. I returned to the rented apartment when I got a call from my sister-in-law that turned the situation south. She started the conversation off with the ever so comforting phrase, "Don't freak out, but your dad was just rushed into an emergency surgery." Apparently, he was hemorrhaging in his C-2 vertebrae where they had put a bridge in between his aging discs. The hemorrhage was found in his post-op MRI, and they could not get the bleeding to stop. In the midst of processing all the information, I was told that he had less than a 30 percent chance of making it through this second surgery, and if he did, he would most likely not walk again. I did the only thing I knew how to do; I fell on my face and cried out to God.

Whether you have a relationship with God or not, He is usually the one most people call upon in circumstances like that. I have been a Christian for the last twelve years and Jesus has become a faithful companion in my life. Sometimes I pray and I am full of faith, and sometimes I pray because I know it's the right thing to do. In this moment, I prayed because I needed a miracle. My family needed a miracle. Something rose up in me that day as I dropped the phone and fell on the floor in tears in my room. I told God over and over through sobs and short breaths that this was my father and no one was going to take him from me. I wholeheartedly believe that prayer changes things, and I needed God to step in and change the situation.

It did not take long for me to decide I needed to go home. I had my ticket changed immediately, not knowing if my dad was going to be alive when I arrived. It was an excruciating 30-hour journey to the Providence, Rhode Island, hospital where my family was waiting. My bags were packed within fifteen minutes of the phone call, and I caught the last flight out of the South Island.

I arrived to find my father still alive; we got a miracle that day. My dad spent seven hours in emergency surgery and came out on the other side, and our family spent the next five days in the ICU awaiting any motor function to return. Much to everyone's surprise and relief, his movement started to come back fairly quickly. The first day he could not breathe on his own, but after five long days, he was able to move his feet on his own. He spent the next six weeks in an intensive rehab facility learning every normal activity that life requires and improved daily.

*"It is often external circumstances
that lead us to internal change."*

Looking back, I realize that was really the moment my season changed, and like most season shifts, the timing and circumstances were not something I would have chosen. The change was bigger than the situation with my dad. I found myself thinking about my own life and the decisions and situations I would need to make.

Life-and-death situations often produce some self-reflection. Processing through what my family went through in those subsequent six weeks from my dream, I found I could now see many things in my life that needed some TLC; some areas of my life were stalled out and some were downright broken down. It is often external circumstances that lead us to internal change. I recognized the change of season, but I could not quite recognize what type of season it was. The dream echoed in my heart still and the phrase "The reward for fruitfulness is pruning because it is your path to even greater fruitfulness," became imminent. A season of loss, self-reflection, and healthy introspection began. What would that process look like for me? That process would look like pruning.

## PRUNING

Pruning is another principle that we see in nature that can be applied to our lives. I purchased a new-to-me home in 2016; it is a ranch-style house on a half-acre of land. I love the house because it is an older home that was fixed up, so I did not have to make improvements. The older home also came with something that homeowners love to call "mature foliage." Basically, it means the property comes with mature and fully-grown trees.

I quickly found this "mature foliage" needed some TLC. It had been there for over thirty years, growing and changing. It made me think about my "mature foliage" being highlighted and needing some attention in my own life. Things that appeared attractive at first glance were found to need attention upon some inspection.

The trees at my house were huge—a mix of redwoods, crepe myrtles, giant overgrown rose bushes, and oleanders. It was evident that some of these trees had not been touched in years; and at the end of the four-year California drought, it was quite possible some of them were not going to make it. The more I got into it, the more I saw how tattered things were. I had roses budding on the end of four-foot leafless branches. Over half the branches on the trees were lifeless. What were once beautiful showpieces became sad and overgrown. I knew if I wanted to see them in their former and perhaps greater glory, I was going to have to clean them up, and by clean them up I mean prune them like crazy.

---

*"I was willing to wait for the seasons of bareness to enjoy the season of fruit again."*

---

I went to work reshaping things as best I could while snip, snip, snipping away. As I filled bin after bin with yard waste, I reflected on my own season. Things that took a lifetime to grow were cut back to their roots. I knew that pruning these trees would make them look exposed and bare for a season. I was willing to wait for the seasons of bareness to enjoy the season of fruit again because I knew it would happen. It is how pruning works. I reflected on the irony of it all as I was rounding out my thirty-third year of life; I realized my house was built the same year I was born. Pruning seemed to be happening for both of us at the same time.

Things sometimes look great from afar; I know these trees did. I spent several days wondering what I was thinking to begin the pruning process. Once it was started, I couldn't stop in the middle without destroying the entire ecosystem created by the trees. It is not much different when we have our lives pruned. Some would say, "Wow, how nice and mature and established you are," but once I got close I realized that much like the branches I was cutting back, I needed to be cut back so I too could grow again. On the inside, I maxed out what my branches could hold through years of neglect. I was fruitful for a season of life, but if I wanted to grow more, I was going to have to take a step back to go forward.

The quote echoed in my heart again: "The reward for fruitfulness is pruning." I was starting to be okay with it now. My heart was positioning itself for the new season, and I was okay with building for the future. I knew what season I was in and I was ready to engage it. Pruning had started as I took inventory of my life, dreams, emotions, hang-ups, and all the areas that came to mind. Month after month of pruning was starting a "remodel" of my inner world. Mixing the metaphors helps to describe what happened next, what the dream spoke of.

## REMODEL

Remodels are often expensive, time-consuming, and extremely inconvenient. Yet, they are often championed when completed. Something gets reconfigured to meet the new purpose and something that was worthless becomes valuable again. Though wonderful when completed, often the inhabitants live in a makeshift home until the work is done. They often live for months without the normal conveniences of a home, such as a kitchen, working electricity in every room, and in extreme cases, a decent place to sleep. Having camping-style kitchens in place of stoves and jugs of water in place of running water is all great in theory and worth it, but sometimes in the process it gets frustrating.

> *"People don't like the work required for change, but everyone loves transformation."*

People don't like the work required for change, but everyone loves transformation. Pop-culture television tells us this. Who doesn't love the show *Fixer Upper*? They take something that is borderline deplorable, often ugly and hopeless, and turn it into a beautiful home that any of us would gladly move into. We see small snapshots of the demo day, the blood sweat and tears it took to get there, all within the hour allotted for the show. The reality is that it takes a team of people, money, and months to complete. Not everyone has the courage to sign up for that type of risky investment, but it is a transformative process that is always worth it. You can see it in the teary reactions at the reveal at the end of every show.

Redemption is a beautiful thing and often enjoyed by those who are willing to endure change. We can accept change better if we see the vision and promise of transformation.

In short, this was a season of great loss for me; in turn, I have seen the most personal growth I have ever experienced. If growth and progress are how I measure success, then this season of external loss or pruning has brought me more inner success than any other season of life. These are some of the keys that have helped me weather the storm and manage change.

## KNOW YOUR SEASON: DEMO DAY

It is impossible to thrive unless you know what season you are in. Is it time for pruning or are you planting something new? Is the house turnkey and ready to go, or is a remodel required? Demo day sometimes requires the most physical effort in a remodel. You are tearing things out and getting to a place where you can start to conceptualize the future product. All the underlying defects are exposed and plans are made to restore and replace them. Much like pruning, it can be a harsh reality but it is always worth it in the end. Identifying the season helps you to embrace the process.

Demo day is often messy, and there is no need to make things look good and get rid of the dust if you are just going to keep tearing things up. There is no need to bring in the finish carpenter when you are still using a sledgehammer. Another word for change is messy; you have to be okay with not having it all together in this stage. It is humbling to have people stop by your remodel and let them see that you have nothing in order. Even worse, things that seemed perfectly good are no longer there. The people who you let in on this stage of life will be the people who celebrate your growth with you. Those same people who saw you when your walls were torn down to the studs will be in awe of what you have done with the place when you are finished with the process.

Knowledge is power and knowing your season is one of the most important things you can do. It is easier to endure and you can even thrive in that place. In a place of knowing your situation, it will help you to be able to know yourself. Have you ever encountered people who are constantly pointing out how terrible things are? The ones who complain that everyone is out to get them and they have constant conflict that follows them in work or relationships? I often listen to stories and wonder if they are actually the common denominator in their issues— that trouble does not follow them, but perhaps the trouble lies within them rather than with the situations they are in. If this is you, a remodel needs to happen. A leaky faucet may be able to give you water, but in the process, it can create a lot of damage and wastes more water than it puts to use.

*"Being aware of our weaknesses will help us not get sidelined by them."*

If we are able to step back and evaluate what our shortcomings and downfalls are, it can help us move forward more quickly. Being aware of our weaknesses will help us not get sidelined by them. Likewise, if we know our strengths, we can cling to those when things get really uncomfortable. For me, I know that laughter pulls me out of bad situations. If the world is crashing down around me, I can find some joke or something to laugh at and my seemingly bad day doesn't seem so bad anymore. In my knowledge of a situation or season, I find that my choice to engage in the remodeling process is the most important step.

## GET WHOLE INSIDE AND OUT: NEW FIXTURES

When a remodel takes place, I want to be sure that I am installing fixtures that are going to hold up under the pressure of everyday use. There are bargain products that sometimes come with less expense but will break sooner. I need to know that I can put weight on my kitchen counters and they will not break. It is the same with our personal lives. We cannot remodel our inner world and replace broken parts with slightly less broken parts, or leave some and hope the others cover it. The better the products we use, the longer the repair will last.

Having my personal life whole makes my performance as an athlete significantly better. There is no way to separate my sports- performance thinking from my personal life. I have been working with a sports psychologist for the last six years. It has been one of the best investments I have ever made in my career. While there are great examples of how she has helped me in the moment succeed in my contest, we actually spend most of the time talking about my personal life and inner process and struggles months away from an event. When people ask me how she most helps me at events, I often think it is the time spent before the event, days processing life's ups and downs, that helps me be the most effective athlete when a contest is on the line.

High-pressure situations bring out the real you; I often see this in big events. If the real you has broken spots in it, it will come out when you apply pressure. We have opportunities to take advantage in seasons of remodeling to evaluate the broken spots in life. Insecurities and low self-esteem are not often seen when you are standing in the winner's circle, but they are identified best when you are not succeeding and are frustrated with circumstances. They come out in moments of pruning or demolition.

Our thinking and our perceptions are the framework that we build our life and dreams on. Think of them as the studs in a remodel. If the studs are rotted out and new support beams need to go in, now is the time to address it.

## CHECK YOUR MOTIVES: FOUNDATIONS

We all know how important the foundation of a house is. Most people won't even buy a house to remodel if the foundation is bad. Foundation problems are difficult and costly to fix and anything you build rests on and is dependent upon the strength of the foundation. The integrity of a house rests on the strength of its foundation. Much like a home, I find that the integrity of our lives rests on our motives. I have also heard it said that "we are at our dumbest when we think we know the motives of others." This is a very personal issue and evaluation.

*"I find that the integrity of our lives rests on our motives."*

Motives, ideas, and thought processes are so important. Most Olympians work on the physical aspects of their sport but fail because of a lack of the mental and internal strength. Just like our bodies need conditioning, so do our inner thoughts and thought processes. These grow, change, and are at times tested. These thoughts are revealed in the size and stature of the things that we can grow in our lives. If we have cracks in our foundation, then what we build will be vulnerable and unsustainable in the years to come. We may even have moments of greatness, but faulty foundations always reveal themselves.

When I experience heart checks, I am always aware that my foundation is being exposed and I can see what I am building on. Although they can be uncomfortable, I am always thankful they come along. Heart tests are seen best by our reactions. Our actions will always show us what we believe to be true. They either leave us pleasantly surprised or slightly embarrassed that we responded that way—there is never a middle ground.

We have to pay attention to the fact that motives can and do change.

*"You can always see your motives when
others succeed and you come up short."*

I will constantly check my heart to make sure it has not slipped into any kind of self-serving or jealous motive. I can tell really quickly if my motives are pure by my reaction to someone else's victory. You can always see your motives when others succeed and you come up short.

## SETBACKS

Disappointment will come no matter how prepared you are. Without fail, all the good home-improvement shows have some type of unforeseen setback. They highlight these setbacks and often make them a focus of the show because setbacks create a dramatic experience for the viewer. You almost wait for it watching the show and they do a commercial break to amplify the drama of it all. What happens at the reveal though is often abundant joy, and the very setback that caused pain and frustration is their favorite part of the house.

If you are alive, I am sure you can relate. Setbacks cannot be avoided. The best we can do is budget for it on the front side. Set aside some heart and brain space to tackle unforeseen obstacles that inevitably arise. Making a plan before you need it is the definition of a plan. Deal with your setbacks while you have the walls torn down, and fix things correctly, even if it costs more than you anticipated. It may be disappointing and cost you for a period of time, but it will be worth it.

It is realistic to get disappointed, but you don't have to stay there. A good way to combat this is to be faithful. I often describe success as faithfulness. When people ask me if I am disappointed after a poor finish at an event, I look back and see all the work I did prior to the competition. If I was faithful with it, took advantage of it, and did my part, then I can free myself up from taking on that disappointment. Sure, I felt disappointed, but I did not enter nor camp in an identity of disappointment.

Take advantage of the opportunity to build things correctly the first time. While things are a mess, invest more than you thought and do it correctly; you will be grateful down the road that you don't have to tear out a wall again.

## HEALTHY MINDSETS: BUILDING PLANS

We engage seasons of change just like we do when we are goal-setting. We do it with a plan and a purpose. No one demolishes a kitchen without having vision of how it can be remade into something better than what was originally there. Developing mindsets in our lives is kind of like sticking to the blueprint. We need those things set up ahead of time and established so we can stay the course in seasons of loss and change. There is the manual labor to be done in the remodel, but it is pointless to tear things up unless you know what you are building.

*"What you build in the dark will be what supports you when it is time to shine."*

It takes both the physical and mental aspects to be successful. You cannot triage mental processes in the moment and expect to have exceptional results. The mindsets you develop in the remodel will be the lens you look through and will sustain you when you need to be at your best. What you build in the dark will be what supports you when it is time to shine.

My sports psychologist always tells me that, on contest days, "It is my job to make it look easy." What I do is far from easy, and it requires so much continual investment. We watch the Olympics and say, "Wow, that person won gold hands down; they made it look easy." We often forget the four years and often a lifetime that was spent getting to that point. I have learned that if you don't have it by the time you get to the Olympics, you won't get it when you get there. What you put in at the beginning and in the process is what you will have manifest in the finished product.

I spent years learning to look at terrible situations as opportunities to learn, grow, and overcome. When things went south at the biggest moments in my career, that was my mindset: "What an opportunity!" When the rubber hit the road, I had nothing but opportunity.

## GRIT

We cannot make decisions based on what we feel. Committing to a process is a choice; you don't always want to do it. Who wants to get up early and ride a dark icy halfpipe or put their life on display and face criticism in the media? Who wants to throw their body in the air hoping to land a new trick but knowing they won't land it the first 100 times? You have to choose to see value in the potential and build intentionally to get somewhere. A person with grit is someone who is tough and courageous. True grit is found in someone who does not let their feelings dictate the choices they make when they are pursuing a goal.

Getting pruned or dropping into a remodel season takes endurance. You often hear of remodels taking much longer than scheduled, and more often than not they cost more than projected. Even when I know I am in seasons of process, I often just expect it to be completed. Remember what you are building; keeping that big-picture perspective will help you grit out the uncomfortable day-to-day situations.

## ENJOY THE PROCESS

Process is a funny thing. Yes, we sign up for remodels after we weigh the cost. Pruning requires something similar to surgery. When you prune a bush, you cut off a branch so the tree can be healthy. If you go to the doctor to get your appendix removed, it is for the good of your entire body. Whether we have voluntarily signed up for a season of change or we find ourselves missing a metaphorical limb, we must embrace it for the promise of growth and transformation. There are some things you can only get through process, and the promise and hope of change for good keeps you alive in the hard times. It gives you perspective to understand the value of what you are learning.

*"There are some things you can only get through process."*

The major hip surgery that set me back a few months is a great example of a difficult process of pruning. I could not get out of bed by myself for the first month after surgery; I needed help with life's most basic functions. Sometimes it seems like a bad dream, and other times I can only see how far I have come.

It was a long process of healing. I knew I would get better but I couldn't do anything to speed up the healing. I understood that the following winter, in all possibility, may be a building block for the Olympic season. I could not gauge how I healed up, or if I would be confident and ready to be highly competitive this season. I went into the next snowboarding season knowing what season I was in. I was most likely still going to be recovering and building. If I did not know what season I was in, I would be setting myself up for a discouraging year. Knowing what season you are in and how it relates to your process will help you be successful.

My endless days of rehab and workouts were actually enjoyable in their own way when I got that big-picture perspective. I was actually embracing the steps along the way because I knew that this process would help me achieve my end goal of a fifth Olympics. In the years to come, I am going to need this, so I put the work in that was required. Whether it is a six-inch box jump or learning a trick that has never been done before, a strong foundation is required.

## THE FINISHED PRODUCT

Life is an eternal process. We have different seasons, but process and change seem to be continual and continually changing. It's just like being a homeowner; there is always a to-do list. Change is the one constant in life and embracing it will help us grow more than we ever expected. If we are growing, we are inevitably going to succeed. When you get to the finish of a remodel, you feel accomplished and delighted. At the same time, you are also aware that the remodel you did this year won't last forever. You can enjoy the season of enjoying the finished product with an understanding that in that enjoyment you are also banking energy, resources, finances, and strength for the remodel required down the road. You learn and grow with each remodel, and the reality is that we never arrive at a finished building that will last forever, and our arrival date in life happens the day it ends.

## REFLECTION QUESTIONS

*Does your current season need a remodel?*

*What sacrifices or pruning will that require?*

*Is it worth it to you?*

2014 · Mount Hood, Oregon

# CHAPTER TEN
# CONSISTENTLY AUTHENTIC

*"We are what we repeatedly do. Excellence, then, is not an act but a habit."*

*–Aristotle*

I have a high need for authenticity. I strive for it in my own life, and I am drawn to it in the world around me. Apart from being authentic, it will be hard to find consistency in your life. Authenticity is impossible to achieve if you don't know who you are or what you value. As I have referenced throughout this entire book, the one constant in our lives is change, so it could seem a bit strange to put such an emphasis on consistency. I want to illustrate a value for it, as it is one of the most important core values I have. I want to live a life of consistency, which may seem humorous because I work in a competitive sports world that is highly inconsistent. I don't strive for consistency out of a need to control things; I love consistency because it allows me to be me in the midst of whatever circumstances I am in. I can live on purpose, and consistency helps me measure success. It gives me a baseline normal. It is the key to living a life that is balanced and sustainable.

My hip surgery was one of the most world-shaking events I have ever experienced. It caused me to reevaluate and reassess what I was doing and why I was doing it. In hindsight, I am thankful for that time and what it produced in me. In the midst of it, I had many unknowns and I had a lot of people inquiring if I was worried about returning to my previous level of snowboarding. As difficult as it was to admit, the answer was yes, I was worried. The time post-surgery was my longest time off of snow in the history of my career; I had not spent that much time away from the hill since I was a kid. Two months off snow is a long stretch for me, so anticipating a minimum of six months away seemed unsettling at best. Getting back on snow after my surgery finally came after seven months of extensive rehab. It was a moment that tested more than my body.

> *"When you do something consistently, you develop the ability to do it with little mental energy."*

At first, I was freaked out, wondering if I would even be able to make a simple run down a hill. My mind went a thousand directions, and then I remembered all the years spent on snow. Up to this point, I have been snowboarding for twenty-five years. I have been snowboarding longer than I have been able to legally drive, so it is laughable to even have the thought that I would not be able to remember how to snowboard.

Along with change, snowboarding has been the only constant in my life. I do most of it without thinking now because of how many days I have spent on the hill. I don't think about how I am going to get my foot in my binding or how I am going to get off the lift. My legs know how to move, absorb bumps, and how to generate speed without a thought. When you do something consistently, you develop the ability to do it with little mental energy. It becomes second nature and your default response to the stimulus.

Consistency is not something that is championed in our culture. We champion achievement while highlighting people's inconsistencies when they make mistakes in life. When I went on some of my winning streaks in my competitions, it was almost more exciting when I would falter and not keep the winning streak alive. It would be more exciting if I were to fall than if I were to win again. Why was that? Because consistency is not exciting from an outside perspective.

If we look at a few of the words to describe consistency, we find words like *tenacious, dedicated, trustworthy, reliable, enduring*, but we also find words like *tedious, mundane, predictable* and *boring*. I want to be enduring, but I don't necessarily want to be mundane or boring. It is a fine line to walk and I can see why it is not attractive at first glance. No one wants to be irrelevant or boring, but we do want to be reliable and trustworthy. It all depends on perspective.

## BEING YOU ALL THE TIME

Whether we would like to admit it or not, everyone has off days, and we usually classify them as "I don't know. I just do not feel like myself today." Like most people, I perform best when I am feeling like myself. We say things like, "I was just on today," or "I felt like a million bucks." Those sayings have been the responses and hallmark of some of my greatest performances—the moments when I was just getting to be me. There is a certain amount of freedom that comes when you feel able to be the genuine you in every moment. Displaying our true selves in the purest forms, no matter the situation, is a very freeing experience.

While we can't control what people think of us, we get to choose whether or not we are going to let their opinions matter more than our desire to be authentic. A big need we have as humans is to be known and ultimately accepted for who we are. That desire cannot cost us the most important thing: our individual identity. Most of us spend a good deal of energy trying to be someone else, but what would your life look like if the real you showed up all the time? I believe it would be a lot less work for starters.

---

*"I want to be the same person whether
I am winning or losing the event."*

---

The journey of really being you all the time starts with finding out who you are, and then committing to be that person in every circumstance. I want to live a life of consistency in which people experience me the same in every situation. I want to be the same person that I am at home as I am at the top of the pipe getting ready to drop in. The same Kelly needs to show up for my friends as the one they see in a television interview. I want to be the same person whether I am winning or losing the event, whether I have a good day or bad day. I want to develop who I am and live that life out.

In doing this, it shows you are a person of integrity. Integrity and consistency go hand in hand. A life of consistency usually leads to a life of integrity when that consistency is applied to something positive. Integrity that comes this way gives you the ability to say something and follow through with it. It makes you able to stand against a flaky culture or one full of compromise. While others might compromise, your integrity allows you to stay away from the trap of being someone who says one thing and does another. Integrity is a crucial aspect of consistency.

## NO COMPARTMENTALIZATION

It is so easy to compartmentalize life. If people can separate the reality of their worlds, it gives the impression that they are in control. While this seems like a good idea, it is not helpful in the big picture, and it doesn't help you live well. There is a difference between doing well in life and having a life well lived. Having the goal to live life well helps us to be authentic and consistently requires a de-compartmentalization of life. It is a key in being able to be you no matter what the circumstances are.

When you compartmentalize your life, it is easy to wear different hats in different situations. Being adaptable is something that is required of us at times. While good in certain moments, it is not something that is always beneficial. When you start to compartmentalize your life, you can easily make up guidelines on how to act and respond in different circumstances to evoke acceptance or a certain response from the people you are interacting with. It can draw you away from your core values. This compromise of sorts leaves you open to be impacted by the world around you because you don't have established guidelines to direct your decisions.

It is easy to see when observing social behavior. It is seen with athletes when they think that rules and sometimes even laws don't apply to them. If you have ever seen the show *Punk'd*, it puts this principle on display, celebrities and athletes alike trying to get out of unreasonable situations by dropping their name and credentials. These are often extreme examples, but it illustrates the principle well. I have a friend who actually got *Punk'd*. A street performer was entertaining him and the "cops" showed up because the street performer had a history of so-called "illegal activities." My friend was "fake" arrested for participating in the ordeal. Without even hesitating, out of his mouth popped his Olympic credentials as if they would get him a literal "get out of jail free" card. I don't know what I would do if I were in this situation, but I know that it is tempting to put away all that we believe in for the easy way out.

Being consistent starts with the establishment of core values in your life—things that are nonnegotiable regardless of what is going on around you. These core values are choices you decide to make before you get into a situation where you might be required to make a quick, difficult choice. Your core values will be determined by a number of

---

*"Situational compartmentalization
steals from you and creates compromise."*

---

things and can be a simple character trait or a statement of purpose about an area of your life. One of my simple core values is to be kind to people. It is very simple, but it is the cornerstone of who I am and who I want to continue to be.

Situational compartmentalization steals from you and creates compromise. You have to know what it looks like in different everyday situations. Let's take my core value to be kind and apply it in multiple scenarios. What does it look like when the airline loses my bags? What about when someone cuts me off on the highway? When I am doing a favor for a friend and they are late? Basically, I get to choose to inhabit my core value; being kind becomes more important than being right or getting my way. It goes beyond convenience of a moment and takes into account the bigger picture.

As I make decisions, my actions are filtered through the question, "What does it look like to be kind in this situation?" If being kind is important to you and part of your core, your question simply becomes, "What does it look like for me to be me in this situation?" You don't have to think about what you would do when you are wearing certain hats or when certain people are around, you simply make a choice in accordance with your values.

The effects of compromise in this area are long-term and hard to undo. It is possible, so don't give up if you find yourself so compartmentalized that you are wondering if you have multiple personalities. People want to know the real, authentic you. They want to see you the way you really are, not a cheap imitation of someone else, trying to convince everyone that you are "cool" or "enough." Find out what your core values are and live them in every part of your life authentically. In doing this, no situation or circumstance will be too much to change who you are.

## LIVE ON PURPOSE

Circumstances cannot dictate your reality or your choices, no matter how difficult they may be. A good way to tell if you are really living a life of consistency is to see how circumstances affect you. As a Christian who is a professional athlete, I often get questions about my faith. The main inquiry is around what it is like to be a Christian in the world of snowboarding. Dozens of times a year the conversation goes something like this: "How does that work? The culture you are in is very different from the culture and values you carry. How do you keep your beliefs and values intact in a place where others don't share the same values?" It is a good question because it is hard for people outside my world to understand. I do value different things than a lot of people in my profession. For instance, my idea of fun is very different at times than others, but it's actually really easy for me to be me and not lose myself in it all. My beliefs and actions are not based on what goes on around me, rather I decided a long time ago my beliefs and actions would be determined by my core values.

One of the traps of circumstantial living comes from people's desire to be loved, accepted, and get needs met. This trap is alluring because when a person is in need, there are things that become options that were not options just moments before. This temptation is huge but must be resisted no matter how lonely or tired we get. I resolved that I won't change what I believe based on what is going on around me to get my needs met in order to up the consistency in my life. It isn't always easy, but I remember a few things: I know who I am and live out of my values to capture my vision and influence the world around me. Remembering what is important makes the temporary pain not seem so painful.

If you ever feel like life happens to you, chances are good that you are letting your circumstances determine your actions. This feeling left unchecked leads to a victim mentality and ultimately a perpetual feeling of powerlessness. You are powerful over your own life whether it feels like it or not. Your feelings are not always truth-tellers. Defeating this mindset by choosing consistency in your core values, choices, thought-life, and resolve will be a battle worth winning. Instead of reacting to situations, you will quickly find that you learn how to respond on purpose. Responding is a sign of intentional decision-making, not being a victim of life.

## CONSISTENCY AND RESPECT

I want to be someone who does what they say they will no matter what. Not a lot of people do what they say they are going to do consistently in our culture. I have found that consistency even on this basic level leads to high levels of respect. Respect cannot be demanded; it must be earned. You will be amazed how people respect and have value for you when you live a life of consistency. Not everyone will agree with you and, believe it or not, not everyone will like you. You will find, however, that because you said something and then you went out and your actions reflected what you said, people will respect you on principle alone. It is admirable and it made them realize they could rely on you, even feel safe around you.

*"Being consistent creates a safe atmosphere for people to exist authentically around you."*

Being consistent creates a safe atmosphere for people to exist authentically around you. People like to know what they are going to get with you and not have to guess which "you" will show up from one time to another. If people know what to expect with you, you are often the person they turn to in times of crisis. When there is a need, you are sought after for advice and input because you are approachable and dependable. Being consistent helps you become an asset to the community you are in and goes beyond having the same set of core values or someone's like or dislike of you.

## A MEASURE OF LONGEVITY

When you decide to live a life of consistency, it is easily measurable over time. It causes you to grow and you can begin to tell how far you have come. Your continual intentional choices create a pathway that shows you where you started, where you are now, and helps you plan for where you can go. When you see growth in your life, you are naturally encouraged and feel good about your process. In the reverse, inconsistency is like trying to plot raindrops on a map; it is almost impossible because you have no grid to go off of to see if you have improved or are falling behind because you haven't tried the same thing more than once or twice. Your choices and reactions to situations are scattered all over the map with no valuable data to extract.

In my life as an athlete, I have found several different exercises and modalities that require consistency or I will lose the ability to do them all together. Pull-ups for me are one of those exercises. It's amazing to see that simply taking a week off from them leads to an inability to do them at all; they simply start to disappear. I have no other type of workout that requires such consistency on my part.

One day, I was really excited because I hit my record numbers for reps and sets. I did three sets of seven and one of six. That is twenty-seven pull-ups in four tries. It may not seem like a lot for some, but I was stoked. My trainer has had me on different progressions with them, and some days I have upwards of fifty pull-ups to complete in a day. I usually find myself nearing fifty by doing sets of one. Shortly after my victory with sets of seven, I got a cold. Right as I was feeling good about the high rep sets, a cold knocked me out for five days of workouts.

---

*"Consistency builds endurance in our lives."*

---

When I finally felt well enough to go back to the gym and jump into my workouts, I quickly found disappointment when I could not get seven pull-ups in a row. Each time, I stopped at five and then they dwindled from there each set to find an ending with ten sets of one. A simple lack of consistency led to a significant downturn in my progress. After a few consistent days and weeks, I was back up. Consistency builds endurance in our lives, and with a little maintenance, we can remain at those high rep numbers.

Consistency over time leads to growth that can be measured. I often get asked in interviews if I am going to slow down with my consistent competitions as I get older in age. This is a legitimate question since I have been competing longer than most of my competitors have been alive. As far as snowboarding goes, I think if I turned my engine off now I would have a hard time getting it started again. I am not sure if I took a long break if I would want to start up again because of all the work it would require to get me back to competition shape. I would much rather keep investing each week in a small way and keep my attention on my progression than pay too much attention to the wins and losses. I remain motivated and encouraged because I see that growth. If I stopped competing for a season, I would probably not have the courage to continue. I rely on the constant encouragement that I get from seeing the growth in my life that consistency brings to keep going. I have a lot I still want to invest in the sport, regardless of how far into my thirties I go.

## BREEDS HUMILITY

I often compare snowboarding to golf. This may seem silly, but I find them similar in nature. In playing golf, you can have an average round, but one perfect shot keeps you coming back for more. Whether it is seeing the longest drive of your life go exactly as planned, or sinking that impossible 40-foot putt, it is captivating. It's that time you hit the pin high off the tee that makes you forget you lost six balls that round. I love snowboarding because it is almost impossible, much like golf. It is hard to be consistent in it no matter how hard you try. One week you land all your tricks and the next you deck out mid-flip and are thankful that the only thing hurt is your pride. The sport has a finish line that keeps moving because there is always room for improvement. It's that one trick that was perfect or that one shot that makes us push on.

I was reading an interview with professional golfer Jordan Spieth after he won the Masters and he made an incredible remark about humility. Someone asked him about his humility and he said, "Me speaking about humility is very difficult because that wouldn't be humility." It struck me as simple yet profound. He continued, "Humility is not something you talk about, it is something that speaks for itself when your life is on display." What do people see when your life is on display?

One of my favorite quotes comes from C. S. Lewis: "Humility isn't thinking less of ourselves, it is thinking of ourselves less." We need to have the balance of a healthy self-view in which we see ourselves as valuable yet not get wrapped up in the idea of getting value from accomplishments. You have to think you are capable and have the ability to be great, but you have to do it with respect and honor for those around you.

*"I never achieve greatness by telling people I am great."*

I have had the privilege of receiving an ESPY nomination on six different occasions. Whether I win or not, I usually go and enjoy getting all glammed up and meeting inspirational sports figures from around the globe. One of the evenings, I was talking with one of the biggest sports agents out there and he stopped and looked around at everyone in the room. He turned to me and said, "We are in a room full of the most accomplished athletes in the world, and you are more accomplished than anyone here. You are the quiet champion." It was one of the best compliments I have ever received. Not everyone would be thrilled to get a comment like that because it is tempting to want the recognition or the attention you have earned. For me, that is not why I snowboard. I snowboard to be the very best me at the highest level, and he affirmed that with his statement. I definitely don't mind the two ESPY awards that I received for my efforts, but that is not what motivates me to be great. Greatness is an inside job and I never achieve greatness by telling people I am great. I get great by putting in the hard work, doing the things I need to do, and not worrying about arriving at the destination called "greatness." This requires a sacrifice and a humility that is hard to put into words.

> *"False humility is good for one thing: keeping you average."*

I never set out to be humble; I set out to be consistent. Setting out to be humble would kind of defeat the purpose. I want to be me in the midst of everything going on around me; I want to pursue excellence and dream of greatness all while not getting my significance wrapped up in my performance. I want to do me really well in a performance culture. I want to have a high value for myself while not letting it consume me or force me to forsake core values for personal achievement. At the same time, I don't want to pretend to be anything, including pretending to be humble. False humility is good for one thing: keeping you average. It puts a lid on your life that only allows you to be as great as what you perceive other people think you should be.

## CONSISTENCY: EVEN IN REST

My family raised me with an incredible work ethic, so unplugging and finding rest are very challenging for me. When I had surgery, I was forced into rest for a season. Prior to this, I consistently worked hard. I just figured working is what you do, and completing a job well is how you do things. While those things are good, too much of any one thing can become a negative thing. Even strengths can be weaknesses if left unrestrained. I had to learn that resting doesn't make me inconsistent, weak, or unfaithful. A rest season actually makes us stronger in the next season if we can embrace it. Even though I learned to rest by being forced to rest, it is also a good idea to choose it on a consistent basis. Rest includes unplugging from the barrage of information filling your mind in addition to the physical rest required for peak physical health.

> *"Even strengths can be weaknesses if left unrestrained."*

What does unplugging look like to you? We have no shortage of information available to us. We have constant feeds of photos, information, thoughts, news, and opinions coming at us and refreshing themselves all day long. What is in your feed? Perhaps a better way to ask it is, what are you feeding yourself with? They don't call it the information age for nothing. While I love the convenience it brings to my daily life, I think we can have too much information streaming at us. Studies have shown that this generation gets more information in a 24-hour period than people in the early 1900s got in their entire lifetime. Think about how that can take its toll on a person when not monitored.

I generally live a very exciting life. I have no issue finding fun photos to post from my travels around the world; photos of snow in summer and beautiful scenic images that would inspire anyone to get outside and enjoy everything that nature has to offer. When I had hip surgery, I found I no longer had an endless supply of images to beam out to the world. Not only did I not have the content, I simply did not have the stamina or brain space to consider being social on social media. I felt pressure to have a presence online, but I knew that would not help in my recovery, so I inevitably unplugged. Surprisingly, I found that it was actually refreshing.

I engaged deeply in the world around me instead of the one on the other end of the Internet. I found it healthy, refreshing, and motivating. I think the common thread here is balance, and I felt like I came back into balance after a break from my phone life. I found other things to focus on, like building things around the house, playing my guitar, reading and taking my pup on adventures. I am now back in the swing of things with my social media life, but things are much more balanced as I stepped back and engaged the world around me. It is important to develop things that you appreciate and enjoy outside of producing things for others to comment on, double click, and swipe. In a way, when we are more focused on how many likes or comments we get, we are spending a lot of time on the end product or destination and not enjoying the process or journey we are on. The pressure of performance is not just found by people like me standing at the top of a halfpipe waiting to drop in. It is found in our daily activities, our ability to unplug and rest and find things that recharge us, allowing us to be us.

In finding myself through a season of rest, I found things that I enjoy or bring me joy apart from showcasing my travels and snowboarding. I rediscovered a love for woodworking and built about 80 percent of the furniture in my home. I took it a step further and started making things for friends. I had more fun going to puppy school with my dog and playing hide and seek with her in the backyard than I would have imagined. I learned how much a dog is good for my heart. Now both of those discoveries have their own social media channels. It is just a broader way for me to authentically share my passions, but they started with me. Once they were passions inside of me, I fostered them, and now I am getting to share them socially. It is all part of the process.

---

*"If you have to promote yourself to get to a position, you have to promote yourself to keep it."*

---

Consistency makes us faithful and dependable. Hard work and consistency naturally produce things. When we are consistent, naturally we grow. I want to always be focused on the progress of things. I never want to work hard to get something for the wrong reasons. If I am too focused and motivated by the accomplishment, then I may have lost sight of the process. It is only a matter of time before the process unravels, and I have become externally driven instead of internally motivated. I have found that if you have to promote yourself to get to a position, you have to promote yourself to keep it. Let the process of progress have its work, and let the achievement be the icing on the cake, not the cake itself. We have to believe that the process is enough and that the things we are dreaming of that have not yet materialized will all be worth it.

## REFLECTION QUESTIONS

*Do you find it hard to be consistent in your daily life?*

*What core values do you live by?*

*How can you grow to be consistently authentic?*

*2008 - Mount Cook, New Zealand*

# CHAPTER 11
# BE INSPIRED

*"Remember why you started..."*

*- Me*

I have always believed that nothing is impossible. This mindset began during my childhood, and I clung to it as I entered my career. Now, it is a cornerstone in my life and has developed into one of my non-negotiables, the backbone of my hopeful, opportunistic approach to life. With this belief as my foundation, it keeps the pursuit of progress ever before me. I don't expect to arrive, so I have stopped trying. I have learned to embrace process and celebrate my progress.

No matter our past, we have the opportunity to develop a new default setting and change the lenses that we view the world through. When I was younger, I wanted to be both successful and significant. I found that the less I focused on myself, the more I saw the importance of leaving a legacy. I find myself approaching the end of an inspiring and fulfilling career, though I believe some of my best moments are yet to come. I still have something to give.

This is a charge to you, to take ownership of your own journey. This is the end of my story as I know it but just the beginning of yours.

## MAY YOU BE HOPE-FILLED AND INSPIRED TO REMEMBER

We have to be a people who ask ourselves every morning what we can give instead of what we can get. We need to be contributors to the world around us and build things that outlast our ability to perform and outlive our current influence. It is time for you to happen to life, and there is something wonderful about pursuing progress with everything in you until you reach your potential.

Growth requires risk; people who never risk often do not grow. If you don't decide where you want to go in life, other people will decide that for you. Make a plan ahead of time and let your actions be dictated by your values and by what you are building. Intentional growth happens because you have a goal.

You are made for process, going on journeys of discovery, and progress. When you raise your own bar, you will in turn free yourself up to take risk. With each step out, the risks become less of a risk. Find the place where preparation and progress meet; it may require courage, but you have what it takes.

*"The journey is the process*
*and the process is the journey."*

You must define your why and work to develop your how. Without a motivating reason behind doing something, you will quickly find yourself in survival mode or wanting to quit altogether. You were meant to thrive in life, not just survive it. Your end motivation cannot be your only motivator. You must learn to embrace the journey. The journey is the process and the process is the journey.

The lens that you look through is very important. Life happens, and it's up to you to decide what to do with it. Choosing to be internally motivated will help you happen to life and not be a victim of it. The only thing that you can control in life is you. When you are internally motivated, you commit to a lifetime of heart tests. When you are internally motivated, you will have many victories, but not all of them will be on display for everyone to see.

> *"The success of others should inspire you, not trigger you."*

Remember, if you are only looking to get recognized for your accomplishment, then you are only building yourself—that is too small a goal. If you set out to enjoy seeing others succeed, then you are creating a legacy that will outlast you. If you are not sure where you are on this spectrum, take inventory when someone around you succeeds and is celebrated—this is the ultimate heart test. How you respond in those types of situations will show you what motivates you. If you find jealousy, comparison, or any number negative emotions, there is probably some work to do in your heart. The success of others should inspire you, not trigger you. With the right perspective, you will not be offended when others are promoted or achieve greater things than you.

Remember, you never actually arrive in life, and seasons can and do change quickly. In that change, you can often feel uncomfortable and vulnerable and you will need to invite others into the process. You will have seasons in life when success is not about medals and victories, but about growing and getting healthy. Keeping a big-picture perspective will help you to adjust your definition of success as seasons change. Be okay with success getting redefined in your life. Success should look beyond the medals and be defined more by your effort and your growth as a person.

Don't ignore performance, but choose not to let it define you. Surround yourself with people who love and believe in you. Success should be distanced from comparison with others and united with the inner motivation to find your best self.

It is easy to mistake success for significance. Our culture tells us that success is the thing that we need the most. Success is not what you most need; significance is what you are looking for. Our greatest human need is significance, and until you can separate your significance from your performance, it is impossible to have lasting, fulfilling success.

When your self-worth is not tied to your winning or losing, you can take bigger risks than you ever considered; because if you dream big and fail, you simply learn a way not to do it the next time. You will have to know what your dream is and what your plan is to get there or you will lose your way when the noise gets loud.

*"Your best is enough and often more fulfilling than all the gold medals in the world."*

Your best is enough and often more fulfilling than all the gold medals in the world. The truth is that after a while they are just more medals, but it is what goes on inside of you that really defines the value of those accomplishments and makes them fulfilling. It is by them that you can really measure if you were successful or not.

Sometimes the one big goal at the end can overshadow the many small achievements that are equally important and necessary. With each completed small goal, we gain strength and courage. The feeling of belief in yourself pushes you to go further and farther; these milestones need to be set out specifically so they can be marked and celebrated.

Growth takes time; it cannot be measured in moments but in seasons. Don't make your goals about something or someone other than you. If

---

*"Take feedback, remain teachable, and find people who put courage in you."*

---

you do this, then you will not be responsible for seeing them through to completion or care to put in the work. You can't control the outcome but you can do your part. In the process, don't forget to let people in to cheer you on and help you steward your dreams. This is an essential element of the process that you cannot ignore. You must have people in it with you to pick you back up when you don't feel like getting up again.

Take feedback, remain teachable, and find people who put courage in you. Those things are essential in the process of life. Find people who are looking to contribute, who want to give instead of get.

Keep in mind that you will often times find what you intentionally look for. No matter what the circumstance, you need to be looking for the opportunity found in difficult situations rather than focusing on the difficulty. You need to always believe and always hope that you can overcome.

Choose a relentless outlook before you need to be relentless. You will often have to overcome your greatest defeat to find true victory. In the rarest form, it will come to light with a reward or a medal, but some of the greatest victories are unseen by others. These internal victories are often more important than the external ones. When you feel afraid, look fear in the face and keep going; do whatever you have to but don't quit. Information and preparation are great antidotes to fear. Fear is not your friend. Love the destination, but welcome the process. That is the best way to grow and conquer fear in all forms.

You cannot hit your full potential if you are motivated by fear. Freeing yourself from what people think about you is not a fun or easy process, but it is necessary. Reminding yourself of what you are building is a good way to defuse this fear. You must have the understanding that your past doesn't have to limit your future. As you celebrate what you did in the past, it can lead you to define what success looks like today. What you build in the dark will support you when it is time to shine. There are some things you can only get through process, and the promise and hope of change for good keeps you alive in the hard times.

*"Greatness is an inside job."*

It is realistic to get disappointed, but you don't have to stay there. A good way to combat this is to be faithful. Learn to define success as faithfulness and free yourself up from taking on that disappointment.

Authenticity is impossible to achieve if you don't know who you are or what you value. Be the same person whether you are winning or losing, whether you have a good day or a bad day. Your feelings are not always truth-tellers; don't let them lie to you.

You are capable and have the ability to be great; do it with respect and honor for those around you. Greatness is an inside job. Champion those around you and celebrate their progress along with your own. Find something to give your life to without letting it define you. Stay inspired, be authentic, and never give up.